STRANGE BUT TRUE VIRGINIA

Strange But True Virginia

Produced by Cliff Road Books

ISBN-13: 978-158173-411-9
ISBN-10: 1-58173-411-5

Design by Miles G. Parsons
Map of Virginia by Tim Rocks

Printed in The United States of America

LYNNE L. HALL

Table of Contents

W. VA.
MD.
VIRGINIA
N. CAR.

In A Strange State:

Road Trip Through Strange But True Virginia

Virginia is for lovers. That's what the Virginia state tourism department will tell you. Visit their state and they promise to show you rolling rivers, charming historical towns, and bustling cities. Read their colorful magazine-style travel guide, watch their slick commercials, and you'll be regaled by the state's many scenic beauties. And, no doubt about it, there are plenty to see.

That's the tourism department's Virginia—elegant, stately, beautiful.

Ahh, but there's another Virginia lurking behind all that beauty and elegance, and it's a state of pure wackiness—a state filled with eccentric characters; crazy happenings; extraordinary, weird, sometimes even spooky, places; and some of the most bizarre landmarks ever built. Forget purple mountain majesties and coastal beauty—we've got Mount Trashmore and mermaids. There are muffler men, giant fruit, dinosaurs, and the world's oldest edible ham. And you just don't want to miss all those weirded-out palaces of collection. Our favorite is the head and neck surgery museum. No end to the fun there!

So drop that colorful tourism brochure. Turn off the pretty commercials. Come tour our Strange But True Virginia. You'll be a Virginia lover in no time!

Strange Statues

We've Got Statues

Strewn across Strange But True Virginia is an eclectic collection of strange and quirky monuments. You'll find a whole crew of muffler men, some really big fruit, giant animals, and the biggest No. 2 pencil you'll ever hope to find.

BIG APPLE • WINCHESTER

There's a giant red apple just sitting in the town square in Winchester—aka the Apple Capital. Surrounded by vast orchards, the town is one of the largest apple export markets in the nation.

Located in Old Town Winchester at the corner of Piccadilly and Braddock Streets.

Winchester honors its history with the Big Apple.
Courtesy of Winchester-Frederick County CVB

BIG PENCIL • WYTHEVILLE

Know how you can never find a pencil when you need one? Well, Wytheville residents never have that problem. They always know where to find a pencil—a really big one.

Seems that back in the 1950s, John Findlay, the original owner of Wytheville Office Supply on Main Street, needed a gimmick to draw in customers (get it? "draw" in...). Anyway, he had a thirty-foot pencil made and stuck it on the front of the business. It's still there—sharpened and ready to write!

Located on Main Street (U.S. 21).

The Big Pencil points customers to Wytheville Office Supply. Courtesy of Stallard Studios Advertising, Wytheville, VA

Crux Gloria Cross • Purcellville

Jesus is on the hill in Purcellville. The Crux Gloria is a thirty-three-foot, seventeen thousand-pound steel cross with a cutout of Jesus in the center. In daylight, both the cross and the image of Jesus are visible. But at night, illumination is such that the cross disappears and just the image of Jesus can be seen.

The cross was fashioned by Virginia artist Tomas Fernandez and was the product of a 1988 dream, in which God appeared to him, requesting that he design a cross with the figure of Christ silhouetted inside. Fernandez complied with the request, and has completed several sculptures that stand on the hill in Purcellville.

Located on Route 7 between Purcellville and Round Hill.

Doughboy Statue • Lynchburg

Lynchburg's Doughboy Statue, also called The Listening Post, honors the past. The bronze sculpture depicts a World War I soldier, rifle in hand, propped casually on a limestone base. Designed in 1926 by Charles Keck, it honors the soldiers who gave their lives in WWI. On either side of the figure are names of men to whom the statue is dedicated.

Located on Church Street at the foot of Monument Terrace.

The Virginia Tourism Department's slogan, "Virginia is for lovers," caused quite a stir when it was introduced way back in 1969. You gotta admit, it's quite a provocative slogan for a state named for England's "Virgin Queen," Elizabeth I.

Francis Makemie Monument • Temperanceville

Francis Makemie was a Presbyterian minister from Glasgow, Scotland, who was ordained in Northern Ireland during the reign of Charles II. He came to the U.S. in 1683 and traveled Virginia, Maryland, the Carolinas, and Barbados, starting up churches all along the way.

Lord Cornbury, the governor of New York, declared Makemie's foreign-earned license invalid and had him arrested for preaching without a license. At his trial, Makemie pled his case so eloquently that he was granted a license and was, of course, released, though not without a stiff fine.

A couple of important things came from this. First, Makemie's exoneration established the extension of the British Act of Toleration, which granted the right of freedom to worship to the colonies. This had a direct influence on the inclusion of the First Amendment in the U.S. Bill of Rights. Second, Lord Cornbury's arbitrary leveling of such an exorbitant amount of money spurred the acceptance of the Eighth Amendment, which states, "Excessive bail shall not be required, nor excessive fines imposed, nor cruel and unusual punishment."

Makemie, known as the Father of American Presbyterianism, is buried in Accomack County, near Temperanceville, and a park has been established at the site. There are park benches and a creek for fishing. A 697-pound bronze statue of ol' Francis himself stands guard over it all.

Located on Monument Road.

Freedom Park • Arlington

Arlington's Freedom Park is home to several icons that symbolize our country's struggle for freedom. The park's main feature is a one-third scale replica of the Statue of Freedom, which crowns the U.S. Capitol. The original Statue of Freedom, sculpted by Thomas Crawford, was placed upon the Capitol dome in 1863, during the midst of the Civil War. The bronze statue is a classical female figure draped in flowing robes, and stands nineteen feet, six inches tall and weighs fifteen thousand pounds. Her right hand rests upon the hilt of a sheathed sword, and her left holds a laurel victory wreath and the shield of the

United States with thirteen stripes. She wears a helmet encircled by stars with a crest composed of an eagle's head, feathers, and talons, a reference to the costumes of Native Americans. A brooch inscribed "U.S." secures her robes, and she stands upon a cast-iron globe inscribed "E. Pluribus Unum."

Freedom Park's clay replica is only seven and a half feet tall but was created to be an exact copy in every other way. Sculptor Michael Maiden says the biggest challenge was sculpting an accurate likeness using just photos and a plaster mold used in the restoration of the original.

Freedom Park honors symbols of the struggle for freedom.
Courtesy of the Newseum

At Freedom Park, you'll also find a toppled and headless statue of Russian dictator Lenin and a bronze casting of the Birmingham, Alabama, jail door that imprisoned Martin Luther King Jr. in 1963.

Currently located at 1101 Wilson Boulevard, but a move to Pennsylvania Avenue in Washington, D.C., is anticipated in 2007.

Giant Gardening Tools • Staunton

The Jolly Green Giant sure is a messy gardener. Seems he left some of his planting paraphernalia strewn across Virginia. In Staunton, he dropped an eighteen-foot tall sprinkler can, a few flower pots, and even his plow. He's gonna need that come spring.

The sculptures were created in the 1990s by local artist Willie Ferguson, who has other large sculptures in front of his business, Ferguson Metal Fabrication.

Located at 765 Middlebrook Avenue.

Giant Gorilla • Virginia Beach

You don't wanna miss out on seeing Hugh Mongous, who's rumored to be a distant cousin of King Kong. A Virginia Beach icon for more than twenty years, Hugh now stands guard over Ocean Breeze Waterpark and Virginia Beach Motor World. You can't miss him. He's a giant gorilla, decked out in sunglasses, a Hawaiian

Hugh Mongous welcomes visitors to Ocean Breeze Waterpark.
Courtesy of Ocean Breeze Waterpark

shirt, and beach shorts. He's also wearing the biggest grin you've ever seen!

Located at 849 General Booth Boulevard.

Giant Milk Bottles • Richmond

Got milk? Richmond's Giant Milk Bottles don't. These days they have tenants. The three bottles once were part of the ol' Richmond Dairy building, constructed in 1913. At a cost of nearly $8 million, the building was recently converted into 113 loft, one-, and two-bedroom apartments. There are even apartments located inside each sixteen-foot milk bottle. Sweet!

Located at the corner of Adams and Marshall.

Giant Pitcher • Lynchburg

For some strange reason, there's a giant pitcher just inside the entrance of the Lynchburg City Cemetery. The ten-foot pitcher, sitting on a brick and concrete base, was a working fountain over the town's water reservoir from 1890 until 1963, when the reservoir was covered. It then stood

A ten-foot pitcher can be found inside the Lynchburg City Cemetery. Courtesy of Southern Memorial Association/ Old City Cemetery

on the steps of the Water Authority for several years before being moved to the cemetery.

Located at 401 Taylor Street.

Facts about Richmond

1. First settled in 1607.
2. In 1780, the capital of Virginia was moved from Williamsburg to Richmond because its position on the James River was thought to be inaccessible to British troops.
3. In 1824, the Marquis de Lafayette visited Richmond.
4. In 1848, Henry "Box" Brown escaped slavery by having himself nailed into a wooden box and shipped from Richmond to Philadelphia. Absolutely, positively overnight?
5. In 1861, Richmond was named the capital of the Confederacy.
6. In 1865, much of Richmond was destroyed at the end of the Civil War, then rebuilt.
7. In 1888, the first electric streetcar system in the United States was started in Richmond.
8. In 1936, the Virginia Museum of Fine Arts was opened, becoming the first state-supported museum in the country.
9. In 1990, Douglas Wilder became the country's first elected African-American governor.

The Homecoming • Norfolk

Norfolk is one of only four cities in the nation chosen to exhibit a statue of The Homecoming, which depicts the reunion of a U.S. sailor with his family following active duty. The bronze sculpture by Stanley Bleifeld shows a sailor in quite an embrace with his wife. The couple's child is hugging them both. It's a celebration of coming home and of the ability all family members have to survive the hardships faced in this time of war.

Located in Norfolk's Town Point Park.

Hot Air Balloon Water Tower • Edinburg

No, that hot air balloon hanging over Edinburg is not full of hot air. It's full of water. It's actually Edinburg's water tower.

Edinburg's water tower looks like a hot air balloon.
Photo by Beecher Bowers

Little Sorrel • Lexington

By all accounts, Little Sorrel was a runty, homely little horse, with a too-thick neck and an undistinguished head. Ah, but beauty is in the eye of the beholder. Despite his undistinguished demeanor, he was the favorite mount of Confederate General Thomas "Stonewall" Jackson. Little Sorrel, whom Jackson also called Fancy, was a tireless campaigner, sometimes carrying Jackson forty miles or more a day. Fearless in battle, he was heedless to the sound of gunfire, and his gait, said Jackson, who was not a natural horseman, was "as the rocking of a cradle." So smooth was his gait that Jackson sometimes fell asleep on his back.

The tough little pony became a favorite of many in the Confederacy as well, with the Southern ladies often running out to snip his mane and tail to braid into wristlets and rings.

Jackson was astride Little Sorrel at Chancellorsville on May 2, 1863, when he was shot by friendly fire. He died a few days later. Little Sorrel was retired to the general's North Carolina plantation, where he was cared for by Jackson's widow until 1883.

Feeling she could no longer care for Little Sorrel, Mrs. Jackson sent him to live at Virginia Military Institute, where Jackson once served as a professor of philosophy and artillery tactics. There, he became a favored pet, reportedly racing around his pasture whenever the cadets fired their rifles. He also would pep up whenever he heard "Dixie" played on the parade ground.

Although he lived his years out at VMI, he was a popular attraction at Southern fairs and Rebel reunions. He also was quite a draw for VMI, where in his later years, too feeble to stand, he would be hoisted on a rig for visitors. Reportedly, a slip from the rig one day resulted in his death. He was thirty-six years old.

Still reluctant to give up their favorite little pony, VMI officials had Little Sorrel stuffed and placed in the VMI Museum, where he stands next to the jacket Jackson wore on that fatal day in Chancellorsville.

Sorrel's bones, which roamed around the Institute in a box, were finally interred to great fanfare in 1997. They are buried on the parade grounds at the foot of Jackson's statue.

Located in Virginia Military Institute on Letcher Street.

MEADE'S PYRAMID • FREDERICKSBURG

Back in 1898, the Confederate Memorial Library Society was looking for a way to commemorate the Confederate soldiers who died in the Civil War. After a flirtation with the idea of wooden signs posted along the railroad (looked too much like advertising), they decided to build a pyramid styled after the one at the Hollywood Cemetery, one of our manmade wonders described in a later chapter.

Guess the good people of the CMLS couldn't raise as much money. Their pyramid, named for General George Meade, is just twenty-three-foot high. It's made of the same dry-stone construction, but seems to be less refined than the ninety-foot Richmond pyramid, more like an ancient Mayan structure.

Meade's Pyramid honors Confederate soldiers who lost their lives during the Civil War.
Courtesy of Fredericksburg Tourism & Business Development

Located just off Lee Drive in the Fredericksburg-Spotsylvania National Military Park at 1013 Lafayette Boulevard.

Mermaids on Parade • Norfolk

There are mermaids in Norfolk! In fact, they're parading around the whole town! It all started in 1999, when Norfolk adopted the mermaid as its official city logo because mermaids, reasoned city fathers, played an important role in Norfolk history. How so, you inquire? Well, we're gonna tell you.

Mermaids abound in Norfolk.
Courtesy of Norfolk CVB

See, legend has it that when a mermaid sheds her scales, they turn to oyster shells. Now, nearby Chesapeake teemed with oysters even before the first English settlers arrived. Throughout the years, the oyster industry has been a major player in Norfolk's economy. And so, to honor the mermaids and thank them for the bounty of oysters, Norfolk has gone just plain mermaid crazy.

Not content to have just one mermaid, in 2000, the town commissioned local artists to sculpt more than two hundred mermaids to be placed throughout the city. Then, in 2005, the city went even crazier. They added five new mermaids and arranged all the maids into a set of three trails that together total a five-mile walk. Lisa Suhey, local author of *There Goes a Mermaid!*, wrote a poem about Princess Azalea, a mermaid in search of her true love. The trails lead visitors on an adventure in search of Princess Azalea's love, with a new stanza of the poem at each stop. There's a different true love at the end of each trail.

The trails are well mapped and take visitors through the town and around the waterfront. Suhey and Norfolk city officials say the trails are a heart-healthy exercise that encourages literacy. We think that sounds a bit fishy, but lots of fun!

Mill Mountain Star • Roanoke

No, that's not a meteorite lighting up the sky on Mill Mountain. It's the Mill Mountain Star, Roanoke's main claim to fame. Originally erected as the world's largest Christmas ornament, the star stands more than eighty-eight feet tall, weighs ten thousand pounds, contains two thousand feet of neon tubes, and uses 17,500 watts of power. It was the world's largest illuminated star until several years ago, when El Paso, Texas, erected a larger one.

Roanoke's star first appeared on the mountain on the eve of Thanksgiving 1949, and it has become an enduring symbol for Roanoke residents, who liked it so much that they decided to leave it up year-round, allowing it to light up the sky until midnight every night.

In 1957, the star became something more than just a

decoration. City officials decided that it should burn red for two days after every traffic fatality in the city. And as the years wore on, this idea was expanded to include national tragedies, such as the assassination of President John Kennedy and the explosion of the Challenger space shuttle.

This neon star has been perched atop Mill Mountain since 1949.
Courtesy of Roanoke CVB/VTC

The star also celebrates the good times, burning red, white, and blue the year of the country's bicentennial and after Roanoke received national honors as an All-American City. Not surprisingly, Roanoke calls itself The Star City.

The star sits inside Mill Mountain City Park, which contains hiking and biking trails and the Mill Mountain Zoo.

Located at the top of Mill Mountain.

MISTY AND STORMY OF CHINCOTEAGUE • CHINCOTEAGUE

Every young girl who grew up loving horses (and there are millions of us) knows the story of Misty of Chincoteague. The book of that name by Marguerite Henry was published in 1947, and immediately became a best-seller. It chronicled the story of

The city limits of Roanoke encompass Mill Mountain, prompting its citizens to claim Roanoke as the only city with a mountain running through it. We can only assume these folks have never visited Birmingham, Alabama, where iron-rich Red Mountain runs right through the middle of the city.

There's another connection between Birmingham and Roanoke: Before being renamed The Star City, Roanoke was known as The Magic City, which is how Birmingham is still known.

the wild ponies of Assateague Island shipwrecked from a Spanish galleon, in particular, the story of Misty, the pony.

Though the book was fiction, it was based on true characters and events. Henry, already a famed children's book writer, came to Chincoteague for the annual Pony Penning, where the wild ponies of Assateague are herded across the channel that separates the two islands. That's when she met Misty, a special pinto pony with markings resembling a map of the U.S. on her side and a blaze down her face in the shape of Virginia.

By promising to include their grandchildren in the book she planned to write, Henry persuaded owners Clarence and Ida Beebe to sell Misty to her. She took the little pony home to Illinois, where she penned the book. After publication, Misty became a celebrity and accompanied Henry on publicity appearances.

After eleven years, Misty was returned to Chincoteague to be bred and raise her foals, the last of which was Stormy, who also became the subject of a Henry best-seller. Misty died in 1972 at age twenty-six, and Stormy followed in 1993. Both horses were stuffed and can be seen at the Beebe's ol' homestead, which has been turned into a museum.

Misty and Stormy now rest in a museum on Chincoteague.
Photo by Amanda Geci

Located at 3062 Ridge Road.

Muffler Men of Virginia

What is this obsession with muffler men? Maybe it's the square jaw. Maybe it's that he's just so darn tall. We don't know, but whatever it is, there are a few muffler men in Virginia to assuage your craving. There's also a Viking and a hayseed thrown in for good measure.

Chincoteague's Viking man gets around. During the 1950s and 1960s, he stood atop a carpet store in Delmar, Maryland. He then moved to an unnamed spot in Crisfield, Maryland, and then on to Marion, Maryland. Finally, in 2001, he settled in

Chincoteague. He's standing in a field on East Side Drive.

Dumfries has a reported real muffler man. But he's not quite so handsome as some of the others. This one seems to be made entirely of real mufflers. He's just four feet tall—a bit runty if you ask us—and he's been painted white.

New Market's guy won't heat up the ladies. He's kinda short—just fourteen feet, and he ain't got no square jaw. In fact, he's pretty goofy looking, what with that upside down pot on his head and a goofy grin on his face. He stands outside the Johnny Appleseed Restaurant just off Route 81, at 162 W. Old Cross Road.

Newport News has a muffler man—wearing a kingly gold crown. He stands outside the Auto Muffler King (hence the crown, no doubt). He's also wearing a red shirt and blue pants and holding a giant muffler in his strong hands. Located at 5835 Jefferson Avenue.

There's a big guy in Roanoke who has stood on the same spot since 1940. It seems the owner of Dabney Tires visited Washington, D.C., for an automotive convention. The big guy was there, stationed in front of the convention center so that visitors had to walk between his legs to enter. Dabney was so impressed that he bought the statue and installed him in front of his store, where he's been ever since.

Today, he stands guard over Williamson Road Service Center, dressed in red and blue and holding an American flag.

Located at 3110 Williamson Road.

PRESIDENTS PARK • WILLIAMSBURG

Back in 2000, Everette H. Newman III somehow hooked up with Texas sculptor David Adickes, who had this great idea for a park full of big heads—big heads of the forty-two (Remember Grover Cleveland served two non-consecutive terms?) U.S. presidents, that is. Adickes convinced Newman that his idea would be perfect for Virginia, what with all those presidents being born there. So, Newman said, "What the hey! Send 'em on." There was just one itty, bitty problemo. Newman neglected to get the permits needed to open a park and to display big presidents' heads.

Presidents Park features eighteen-foot sculpted busts of U.S. presidents arranged in a relaxed garden setting.
Courtesy of Presidents Park/Williamsburg Area CVB

When the first six heads arrived on a flatbed truck and sat discombobulated outside the Williamsburg Days Inn, which was owned by Newman, city officials raised a ruckus. Just what were these big heads doing on that truck? And, what did Newman plan to do with them? What?! A ten-acre park with presidents' heads?! Whaaat?!

Williamsburg muckety-mucks thought the whole idea was

quite tacky and called on York County officials, who effectively blocked the park by requiring expensive special zoning permits. So, of course, Newman and Adickes sued.

The ensuing court battle took four years. In the meantime, the presidents' heads had to reside in temporary digs. Some sat lonely on a hillside in Glen Maury Park in Buena Vista; others found a home at the Norfolk Botanical Gardens.

Finally, the two presidential entrepreneurs prevailed, and in 2004, Williamsburg's new Presidents Park opened, featuring the big heads of all forty-two presidents.

There's a few complaints about the likenesses—some say there's just something not quite right about John Kennedy's face, and maybe George H. W. Bush's, too. But for the most part, the park seems to be taking off nicely, with twenty thousand visitors its first year. There's also a museum on site that houses classrooms and meeting rooms, a gift shop (of course!), café, and banquet rooms.

Located at 211 Water Country Parkway.

Turkeys • Rockingham County

OK, we're not sure why anyone would want to be known as the Turkey Capital of the World, but apparently the title is in great demand. There are, in fact, at least five cities vying for the honor. Rockingham County is the largest producer of turkeys in Virginia and is a major producer worldwide, and so, the good folks there feel they have the legitimate claim. They back it up, too, with matching turkey statues—one at each end of Route 11.

U.S. Marine Corps Memorial • Arlington

This seventy-eight-foot memorial is, no doubt, familiar to every red-blooded American. The bronze statue depicts five Marines and one Navy corpsman raising the American flag atop Mount Suribachi on Iwo Jima on February 23, 1945. Dedicated to all personnel of the U.S. Marine Corps who have died in the defense of the country since 1775, it was inspired by the Pulitzer Prize-winning photograph *Raising the Flag on Iwo Jima* by war photographer Joe Rosenthal.

The U.S. Marine Corps Memorial was inspired by Joe Rosenthal's *Raising the Flag on Iwo Jima*. Courtesy of VTC

The base of the memorial, sculpted by former Navyman Felix W. de Weldon, lists the location and dates of every major Marine Corps engagement. The memorial was dedicated by President Dwight D. Eisenhower on November 10, 1954, the 179th anniversary of the Marine Corps. In 1961, President John Kennedy proclaimed that a U.S. flag should fly from the memorial twenty-four hours a day—making it one of only a few official sites where this is permitted.

Located at the intersection of Arlington Boulevard and Meade Street.

Virginia's state motto is "Sic Semper Tyrannis" (Thus always to tyrants). Hmmm. We're gonna assume there's some kind of arm gesture that goes with it.

Natural and Manmade Wonders

Wackiness abounds on the byways of our Strange But True Virginia, with its weird hodgepodge of natural and manmade wonders. You can picnic at a mountain made of trash, or contemplate the mysteries of life at Virginia's own Foamhenge.

ARLINGTON CEMETERY • ARLINGTON

Arlington National Cemetery is the nation's largest burial ground.
Courtesy of VTC

Arlington Cemetery is the country's largest national burial ground with more than six hundred acres of landscaped hills. Its rows and rows of white headstones are a familiar sight to every Memorial Day newscast. Here you'll find the graves of the country's elite: President John F. Kennedy, Supreme Court Justice Thurgood Marshall, the country's most decorated soldier (and cowboy) Audie Murphy, and World Champion Boxer Joe Louis, just to name a few. You'll also find the Tomb of the Unknowns here.

The place was never meant to be a cemetery. Arlington House, which sits on a hillside overlooking the Potomac River and Washington, D.C., was built by George Washington Parke Custis, George Washington's adopted grandson, as a living memorial to George Washington. Begun in 1802 with the north wing, the mansion was not completed until 1818.

Custis and his wife, Mary, lived in the house the rest of their lives, amassing a large collection of George Washington memorabilia, including portraits, personal papers, clothes, and even the tent Washington used at Yorktown. Both Custis and his wife were buried on the property.

The house passed to the couple's only child, Mary Anna, who had married a distant cousin, a young fellow named Robert E. Lee. The couple lived in the home until Virginia seceded from the Union, and Lee deemed it dangerous for them to remain there. In 1861, federal troops crossed the Potomac and seized lands around Arlington. After the occupation, military installations, including Fort Whipple, now Fort Myer, and Fort McPherson, now Section II, were erected at several locations around the eleven hundred-acre estate.

In 1864, Arlington was confiscated when taxes levied against the property were not paid in person by Mrs. Lee. The property was sold to a tax commissioner for government use. Brigadier General Montgomery Meigs, who commanded the troops occupying Arlington House, appropriated the grounds on June 15, 1864, for use as a military cemetery.

It was Meigs's intention to destroy the house should Lee ever attempt to return. A stone and masonry burial vault in the rose garden was one of the first monuments to be erected. The vault, twenty feet wide and ten feet deep, contained the remains of eighteen hundred Bull Run casualties. Meigs, his wife, father, and son also are buried here—the final statement in his original orders.

After the war, the federal government dedicated a model community for freed slaves, called Freedman's Village, on the property grounds. More than eleven hundred freed slaves were given land, where they lived and farmed.

Lee never tried to reclaim Arlington, though he regretted its loss deeply. After his death, his son, George Washington Custis Lee, sued to have the government ejected on grounds that the land was seized illegally. The Supreme Court agreed, and the land was returned.

That's not the end of the story, however. Custis Lee obviously wasn't as attached to the land as his parents, for on March 3, 1883, he sold the property to Congress for $150,000.

Today, more than three hundred thousand people are buried in Arlington Cemetery, with sixty-four hundred burials conducted annually. Not just any ol' body can be buried here. To be eligible for a plot, you must have been in the armed forces or immediate kin to someone who was, a president or former president of the U.S., a U.S. elected official, or a justice official.

The Tomb of the Unknowns is one of the most visited sites, along with the Eternal Flame of U.S. President John F. Kennedy, the Space Shuttle Challenger Memorial, and the Confederate Memorial.

One of the most interesting sites is the Lockerbie Cairn, which memorializes the 270 lives lost in the terrorist attack on Pan Am Flight 103 on December 21, 1988. The plane was flying over Lockerbie, Scotland, when a bomb exploded in the cargo hold. The Cairn, made of 270 blocks of red Scottish sandstone, was a gift from the people of Scotland to the people of the United States.

Located on Memorial Drive.

Virginia is one of four U.S. states known as a commonwealth. The designation means that these states emphasize that they have a "government based on the common consent of the people," rather than a government legitimized through their earlier Royal Colony status, which was derived from the King of England. The other three commonwealths are Kentucky, Massachusetts, and Pennsylvania.

Bull Run Castle • Aldie

When John Miller says he'll do something, you can count on it. Back in 1986, Miller told everyone he was going to build a castle, right there in little Aldie. And not just one of them showplace castles either. No sirree. His castle would be a "working castle," with multiple gun ports to turn away marauding knights or raccoons, whichever the case may be. It took him nigh on to twenty years, but, by golly, he did it.

Miller started his castle in 1980 in the middle of a former

cornfield. Using recycled materials and just the help of his wife and children, he painstakingly constructed a medieval castle in the middle of the Virginia hinterlands. The wife and children left years into the project, but Miller continued, determined to keep his word.

The castle's architecture is true to medieval form, complete with turrets, a keep, and a dungeon. The décor, however, is quite eclectic, with a suit of armor standing guard over an Egyptian sarcophagus. Modern and antique weapons are juxtaposed with dainty Hummel figurines. There are even a few half-sized Confederate caskets—made to bury legless soldiers! And all of it's for sale in the castle's antique shop. In fact, the whole castle is for sale.

Until such time that it does sell, you can visit Bull Run for a tour by its opinionated builder, a staunch conservative and Republican. And, if you've a mind to, you can even stay in the castle's "romantic" Tourdela Amoire—a small room built inside the castle keep. For sixty bucks, you'll even get a breakfast prepared by Miller, who plans to open up three more rooms for overnight stays.

Located on Route 15 where it intersects with Route 50.

Crystal Caverns at Hupps Hill • Strasburg

Crystal Caverns are Virginia's oldest known caverns. Friendly Shawnee Indians revealed the caverns to the Hupp family in 1755. Millions of years old, the caverns may have served as a den for ice-age predators, such as saber-toothed tigers. They also were used as ceremonial grounds for Native

Americans, shelter for Civil War soldiers, and as a passage to freedom by escaped slaves.

Opened in the 1920s for tours, Crystal Caverns is now a laid-back attraction, where guided tours led by flashlight cover the caverns' geology and history. As you might guess from the name, the outstanding feature of the caverns is the billions and billions of crystals that give the cave a fairy-tale atmosphere. Glinting in the lantern light, they are a popular draw for psychics (Jeane Dixon was a frequent visitor) and New Age folks, who come here to absorb their perceived energy. There are also reports of supernatural presences, ghostly images that show up only in photographs.

One of Crystal Caverns' attractions that you're more likely to hear about than to see is Andy the Amphipod. Andy is an eyeless, colorless crustacean that's found nowhere else in the world. Although his presence was only recently discovered, it's likely that his ancestors have existed within the cave for millions of years.

Crystal Caverns are Virginia's oldest known caverns.
Courtesy of Crystal Caverns

There are guided tours daily. Special candlelight tours

with guides in period costumes are conducted periodically. A spooky haunted tour is held on Halloween.

Located at 33231 Old Valley Pike.

FOAMHENGE • NATURAL BRIDGE

This exact replica of Stonehenge sits on a hill in the midst of the Blue Ridge Mountains. Each stone, says designer Mark Cline, is shaped just like the original—fashioned, as you may have guessed, of foam. To get his exact measurements and designs, Cline consulted with the man who gives tours of Stonehenge in England. He also consulted with a local psychic to place the stones in the correct astronomical alignment.

Foamhenge is a foam replica of Stonehenge.
Photo by Tina Duff

Cline plans to hold celebrations, such as the Summer Solstice, here, but complains of the difficulty in finding local virgins for sacrifice. So beware, young maidens, should you visit at this time!

Located on Route 11, about one mile from the Natural Bridge complex.

GRAND CAVERNS • GROTTOES

Grand Caverns, rated the country's No. 2 cavern by *Parade* magazine, was discovered in 1804 by eighteen-year-old Bernard Weyer, a trapper in search of a lost trap. The cave was opened to the public in 1806 and has been in continuous operation since that time, which, according to the literature, makes it America's oldest show cave.

The giant rooms of Grand Caverns, with such fanciful names as the Tannery, the Lily Room, and the Shield Room, are filled with spectacular formations that cover walls, floors, and ceilings. In addition to stalactites, stalagmites, and the gentle drapery formations that flow down the walls, Grand Caverns is blessed with an abundance of the rare "shield" formations. These thin-disk formations, which resemble dinner plates projecting from walls, ceilings, and floors, are normally found in numbers of only ten to twelve per cave. The shield formations in Grand Caverns number more than 250.

The highlight of the tour is the seven-story-high Cathedral Room. At 280 feet long and seventy feet high, it is one of the largest rooms of any cavern in the East. Also, if you look closely at the walls—but don't touch!—you can find graffiti left there by Confederate and Union soldiers.

Grand Caverns is open to the public April 1 through October 31. During those months, in the park above ground you can also enjoy picnicking, hiking, swimming, and mini golf. The Grand Caverns Bluegrass Festival and Haunted Cave Tours are held there, too.

Located at 5 Grand Caverns Drive.

HOLLYWOOD CEMETERY • RICHMOND

Nope. You won't find the graves of famous movie stars here. But you will find a U.S. president or two, a few Confederate heroes, and, wow, some pretty interesting stuff.

Hollywood Cemetery, named for the many holly trees here, was opened in 1849, and quickly became THE place to be buried. Presidents James Monroe and John Tyler RIP here. So do Confederate President Jefferson Davis, General JEB Stuart, and eighteen thousand Confederate soldiers. There are writers, artists, philanthropists, and Supreme Court justices.

Hollywood Cemetery's most famous—and tallest—structure is the Confederate Pyramid, completed in 1869 by the Hollywood Memorial Association. The women of this association believed there needed to be something to commemorate the Confederate soldiers laid to rest here. They held a two-week bazaar, raised $18,000, and hired artist Charles Dimmock to erect a monument. The pyramid, built over the grave of eighteen thousand soldiers, is made of dry stacked James River granite and stands ninety feet high. War mementos, such as bullets, uniform buttons, worthless Confederate money, and a piece of the jacket that General Stonewall Jackson died in, are secreted inside. Story has it that the placing of the capstone—a dangerous task in those days—won a local prisoner his freedom.

The cemetery was designed during a time when it was believed that cemeteries should be a place for leisure activities, not just a place to bury the dead. In keeping with that grave idea, the 135-acre cemetery winds around in a shady, peaceful loop that resembles a park more than a graveyard.

Located at 412 South Cherry Street.

LURAY CAVERNS • LURAY

The Find of the Century. A Fairyland in Stone. U.S. Natural Landmark. All these phrases have been used to describe Luray Caverns. The caverns were discovered in 1878 by Andrew Campbell, the town tinsmith, his thirteen-year-old nephew Quint, and photographer friend Ben Stebbins, all of whom were out searching for a cave to explore. And, boy, did they find one.

Imagine their wonder when, after four hours of digging away loose dirt, they dropped by rope into the East's largest caverns. All around them, their candlelight cast flickering shadows of huge stalactites and stalagmites.

Luray Caverns are the East's largest caverns.
Photo by Buddy Mays/Courtesy of VTC

The huge subterranean rooms of the caverns contain a wild profusion of formations and colors. In 1880, the Smithsonian Institute reported that no cave in the country contained more stalactite and stalagmite ornamentation than Luray Caverns. Not one inch has escaped adornment.

Every wall is covered in crystalline deposits of flowstone, which form dramatic decorations of draperies, frozen waterfalls, veils, and tents. Natural minerals seeping into the water splash these formations with vivid colors—reds, blacks, yellows, whites, greens, and blues.

While you're marveling over the fantastic natural sights, eons old, you'll find yourself entertained by haunting music of the world's only Stalacpipe Organ, which is also the world's largest musical instrument. Invented in 1954 by scientist Leland Strickland of Springfield, the organ produces symphonic quality music by striking three and one-half acres of the cavern's stalactites with electronically controlled rubber mallets. Strickland spent three years searching out stalactites to perfectly match a musical scale.

Oh, and if exploring the East's largest cavern isn't enough adventure for you, you can also wander through the Garden Maze, one of the largest in the Atlantic states, or see an exhibit of transportation in America at the Car and Carriage Caravan.

Located at 970 U.S. Highway 211 West.

Mount Trashmore • Virginia Beach

You could call Mount Trashmore recycling Virginia-style. It seems that several years ago, Virginia Beach residents had a problem. Not only was the town landfill overflowing, but it also was located too close to residents. The smell was bothersome. What to do?

Hey, let's turn it into a mountain park! We have the technology! We can do it! The trash was compacted with clean soil into eighteen-inch squares with a density of one hundred cubic feet per cubic foot. The squares were placed on top of each other, covered with six feet of clean soil, and compacted further with bulldozers. The resulting mountain is eight hundred feet long and sixty feet high.

A few things were taken into consideration in the building of Mount Trashmore. First, the ground water was analyzed to be sure no contaminates were leeching in. And, oh, yeah. We gotta do something about all that methane. Seems that when garbage decomposes, it forms methane, a flammable gas and the stuff of gastric distress.

The mountain's engineers jammed seven hollow poles into the mountain in strategic places. Now, several times a day, the mountain poots, expelling methane into the atmosphere. Problem solved.

The mountain was completed way back in 1974. Today, it's a full-blown park, with a playground, 1.45 miles of jogging trails, fishing, and picnicking. You can join the more than nine hundred thousand visitors who come here annually to enjoy the park and all its amenities, and if you sometimes catch a whiff of something … you can point a finger at the mountain.

Located at 310 Edwin Drive.

Natural Bridge • Natural Bridge

It's a town! It's a natural wonder! It's a wacky tourist attraction! Take your pick. Natural Bridge is pretty much whatever you want it to be.

More than one hundred million years old, the natural

wonder of Natural Bridge is a natural rock formation that spans a two hundred-foot deep gorge. According to legend, it was first discovered by sixteenth-century Monacan Indians as they ran for their lives, hotly pursued by Shawnee and the Powhatan, when they came upon a deep gorge. It seemed that all was lost. But, what's that? A natural bridge across the gorge. We're saved. Maybe.

The men of the tribe, brave warriors that they were, sent the women and children across first, following only after the bridge's safety had been tested. We understand that the Monacans escaped death that day, though there's no word on why their enemies did not cross the bridge themselves.

Thomas Jefferson purchased Natural Bridge in 1774. It was later sold by his descendants. Courtesy of VTC

In 1750, young George Washington surveyed the Natural Bridge area for England's Lord Fairfax. The landmarks of his work remain, as do his initials where he carved them on the side of the wall. Graffiti was a popular sport even back then!

On July 5, 1774, just before the beginning of the American Revolution, Thomas Jefferson purchased 157 acres of land here, which included the natural bridge, from King George III. It cost him twenty shillings, a bargain even in those days.

Development of the property began when Jefferson built a two-room cabin retreat, one room of which was reserved for guests. His heirs sold the site in 1833, and the new owner, recognizing its potential, built the Forest Inn to accommodate a growing number of guests. By the 1880s, Natural Bridge, under the ownership of Colonel Henry Parsons, attained resort status. It was a popular destination of Europeans during the eighteenth and nineteenth centuries. Today, it remains privately owned. The hotel, built in 1963, features colonial-style décor and spacious rooms. Apart from the main hotel, there are more casual cottages.

From March through November, the caverns are open to visitors. There's also a mile-long nature park, featuring such sights as Saltpeter Cave and Lace Falls.

Tired of nature? Don't despair! You'll find a living history Monacan Indian village, a wax museum, a toy museum, a safari park, and a zoo, among other attractions located in Natural Bridge.

Located on Route 11 between Interstate-81 Exits 175 and 180.

The Pentagon • Arlington

Geez! And you thought you worked in a big office! The Pentagon, headquarters of the Department of Defense, is one of the world's largest office buildings. Built in five concentric rings, the building has more than 6.5 million square feet of floor space, more than 3.7 million of which is used for office space.

The Pentagon serves as headquarters of the Department of Defense. DoD photo by Master Sgt. Ken Hammond, U.S. Air Force

It's a city within itself, with more than twenty-three thousand employees.

The speed of the construction of the Pentagon defied the usual bureaucratic red tape. Back in 1941, the outbreak of World War II had placed tremendous demands on the War Department (now the Department of Defense). They desperately needed more room to plan their strategies. The job of making more space fell to the Chief of Construction, Brigadier General Brehon Somervell, a man of action, no doubt.

Somervell took just four days to develop plans for a new office building—for forty thousand people—with five sides, three floors, and four million square feet of office space. Just months later, on September 11, 1941 (Whoa!), construction began on a former wasteland of swamps and garbage dumps and proceeded hastily. In the meantime, Pearl Harbor was bombed (December 7, 1941), and as a result, two more floors were added to the construction plans. To conserve steel in this time of war, concrete ramps instead of elevators were used to connect the floors. The outside walls were made of reinforced concrete.

Seven months after the groundbreaking, the first two sections of the Pentagon were finished and the War Department moved in. By January 15, 1943, all five stories were finished at a cost of $83 million.

Each ring of the Pentagon is designed to serve as a stand-alone building with its own utility system, a design that lends itself well to renovation, since the building being renovated could be shut down without affecting the other buildings. And renovation is an ongoing process here, to continually strengthen the building with blast resistant windows and steel reinforcements.

Just such a renovation was in progress on September 11, 2001, when the terrorist attacks occurred. The plane crashed into two sections—one of which had just been finished with a sprinkler system and blast resistant windows. The other section had neither a sprinkler system nor reinforced windows.

Because of these renovations, only a small portion of the usual forty-five hundred Pentagon employees was working in these sections, resulting in a much lower number of deaths than would have been expected. On that day, 184 people, including the passengers on Flight 77, lost their lives.

Renovation crews immediately set to work repairing the damage—an undertaking dubbed The Phoenix Project—and the sections were soon rebuilt.

Tours of the Pentagon are available for school, educational, and other special groups by reservation.

Pentagon Facts and Figures

1. The Pentagon building encompasses twenty-nine acres.
2. In addition, there's a five-acre courtyard in the center of the building.
3. There are more than seventeen miles of hallways.
4. There are 131 stairways, nineteen escalators, and thirteen elevators.
5. There are 284 restrooms. That's twice as many as necessary, because Virginia's segregation laws were in effect when the Pentagon was built.
6. More than two hundred thousand telephone calls are made daily through the building's one hundred thousand miles of telephone cable.
7. More than 1.2 million pieces of mail are processed monthly.
8. Clock-watching employees will have no problem knowing when it's time to go home. The building has forty-two hundred clocks.
9. More than forty-five hundred cups of coffee are consumed daily.
10. There are 16,250 light fixtures.
11. The five concentric rings are named A, B, C, D, and E, from the inner ring (A) moving to the outer ring. How inventive!
12. There were 410,000 cubic yards of concrete used in the building, using 680,000 tons of sand and gravel dredged from the Potomac River.

Shenandoah Caverns • Shenandoah

Shenandoah Caverns was discovered in 1884, when a blast during the construction of the Southern Railway allowed vapor to escape from a resulting fissure. Two curious teenagers grabbed ropes and lowered themselves 150 feet to the cavern floor.

At Shenandoah Caverns, American Celebration on Parade features floats from the Rose Bowl and presidential inauguration parades.
Courtesy of American Celebration on Parade

The caverns weren't open to the public until 1922. A hotel, which used the caverns' naturally cool air for cooling, was built over the cavern entrance. The upper floor of the hotel burned in 1957 and wasn't rebuilt, but the first story remains over the entrance and houses the Main Street of Yesteryear, a collection of antique animated window displays.

The proximity of Shenandoah Caverns to the railroad guaranteed a steady stream of visitors during the 1930s and 1940s. Such celebrities as Greta Garbo, President Herbert Hoover, the Astors, and the Vanderbilts all toured the caverns during these heyday years.

A series of "firsts" also took place here: the first movie filmed underground, the first telephone installed underground, the first newspaper story filed from a cavern, and the first elevator installed in a cavern. The elevator was installed in 1932 and was hand dug through sixty feet of limestone. It remains Virginia's only cavern elevator.

OK, enough of that. Let's talk formations. There are seventeen separate rooms in Shenandoah Caverns, most formed by the receding of the great inland sea and violent earthquakes. The formations are so spectacular that they were once featured in *National Geographic*. You'll find the Capitol Dome, a formation that does, indeed, resemble the Capitol Dome; Cascade Hall, a room filled with cascades of calcite crystal formations; The Bacon, formations that were highlighted in *National Geographic*; and many other types of formations.

Don't be surprised if you catch a glimpse of a pixie during your tour. The grinning little imps have been around since the 1960s, when they were first introduced on billboards and logos.

In addition to a tour of the Shenandoah Caverns, you won't want to miss the American Celebration on Parade. This attraction is forty thousand square feet of famous parade floats, props, and settings from major American events and history. There are Rose Bowl floats, presidential inauguration floats, giant buffalo, elephants, and cowboys.

Located at 261 Caverns Road.

St. John's Church • Richmond

Built in 1741, St. John's Episcopal Church is the oldest church in Richmond, but that's not why we're including it in our tour. We're including it because an important piece of American history occurred here on March 23, 1775. On that date, the church hosted the Second Virginia Convention, which was attended by Thomas Jefferson, George Washington, and a fellow known as Patrick Henry. The debate that day centered around the need to raise a militia to resist the encroachments of the British government upon the civil rights of the colonies. Henry delivered some fightin' words that day, words that to this day fill the hearts and eyes of every American:

> Is life so dear, or peace so sweet, as to be purchased at the price of chains and slavery? Forbid it, Almighty God! I know not what course others may take; but as for me, give me liberty or give me death!

Hearing the speech, the crowd rose to its feet with cries of "To Arms! To Arms!" Henry is credited with single-handedly convincing Virginia to enter the Revolutionary War.

Although it's an active church, tours of the churchyard, where many prominent Richmond citizens are buried, and the church are conducted regularly. You must sign up in the souvenir shop, located within the churchyard. Public and private reenactments of the Second Virginia Convention are also offered.

Located at 2401 East Broad Street

Stone Face Rock • Pennington Gap

Just north of Pennington Gap, off U.S. Highway 421, is the Stone Face Rock, a prominent rock outcropping that looks like a huge head and face. The formation is a result of erosion by the Powell River flowing over the gray sandstone. Although it has been suggested that the face was possibly carved by Native Americans, who considered it the entrance to their holy grounds.

Westmoreland Berry Farm • Oak Grove

Look! Up in the air! It's a bird! It's a plane! No, it's a goat! What? You didn't know goats could fly? Well, actually, they can't. But they sure can climb. Seeing a goat in the air is a common occurrence at the Westmoreland Berry Farm.

Seems that back in 2000, the owners, perhaps needing something spectacular to draw in customers, anchored wooden platforms and boxes to twenty-foot tall poles. They then connected them to the ground and each other with a series of narrow wooden ramps. And, voilà! The Westmoreland Berry Farm Goat Walk.

While looking at goats sunning themselves twenty feet above you might be all the excitement you need for one day, there's more to be had! You can actually feed these high-flying critters. Just drop a quarter into the feed dispensing machine, and the goats come to life. Faster than a speeding bullet, a goat reaches the feeding station, and impatiently stamps and butts while you clumsily place the dispensed corn into the little feeding bucket and hoist it on high. The goat gobbles up his treat, then returns to his sunning. Wow!

OK. That was fun. But there's even more to do here. If it's harvest season—April through October—you can pick your own fruit and vegetables to take home. If that's not your idea of fun, however, you can purchase already picked items, including strawberries, raspberries, pumpkins, peaches, and apples. Then you can enjoy Westmoreland's famous strawberry shortcakes or sundaes in the shade, picnic on their hot dogs, chips, and drinks, or even sample a bit of goat's milk.

Adjoining the farm is the Voorhees Nature Preserve, which offers four miles of scenic trails along the Rappahannock River. This is a bald eagle nesting place and, though the nesting area itself is off limits, you have a good chance of seeing one of these majestic birds soaring overhead.

Located at 1235 Berry Farm Road.

World's Oldest Edible Ham • Smithfield

Oh, yuck! Talk about hammin' it up! The town of Smithfield boasts of having the world's oldest edible ham. Now that doesn't sound all that yucky until you learn that the ham in question has been around since 1902!

It seems that back then, P. D. Gwaltney Jr., the owner of a mercantile that sold hams, discovered the ham, which had been overlooked in a delivery several years before. Noting that the ham seemed to be still edible, he decided to find out just how long the ham would last. You see, it was a Smithfield ham, which, because of their processing, keep indefinitely without refrigeration.

Remember that story about Captain John Smith and Pocahontas? Didn't you wonder if it was true? Well, it was.

Smith, who was serving as president of Jamestown, was leading a food-gathering expedition up the river, when he and his men were attacked by Native Americans. When all his men had been killed, Smith strapped his Native American guide to himself as a shield. The ploy worked, and he was captured by Chief Powhatan's half-brother, who, for the price of a compass, decided to let Smith live.

Seems the chief's bro didn't have the last say in the matter, however, because when Smith came before Chief Powhatan, the chief decided to execute him. The execution never took place, though. The chief's comely daughter, Pocahontas, took a liking to Smith and pleaded for his life. Softie that he was, Chief Powhatan relented, and Smith lived to write about the incident later.

Contrary to what many believe, that was Pocahontas's only encounter with Smith. She did, however, develop a lasting relationship with the English. When Jamestown was destroyed by fire in the winter of 1608, she brought food and clothing to the colonists. She later negotiated with them for the release of captured Native Americans.

In 1614, her relationship went even further. She converted to Christianity, took the name of Rebecca, and married settler John Rolfe. The couple moved to London in 1616. They returned to Virginia in 1617, but Pocahontas died shortly after their arrival.

Gwaltney's ham was featured in Ripley's Believe It Or Not as the world's oldest ham, and Gwaltney even insured it for $1,000, which, of course, he never collected upon, because the ham outlived him!

Now more than one hundred years old, the ham resides in a glass case in Smithfield's Isle of Wight Museum. Though advertised as "edible," it doesn't seem to have aged all that gracefully. It's green and shriveled. We're thinking you should probably eat before you go.

The Isle of Wight Museum is located at 103 Main Street.

YOGAVILLE® • BUCKINGHAM COUNTY

Yogaville® is a community that lies in Buckingham County. Dedicated to the teachings of Integral Yoga®, it was founded by Sri Swami Satchidananda, founder of Integral Yoga® International, a major Yoga tradition.

LOTUS is the first shrine in the world to house altars for the world's major religions. © Yogaville®

Seems that back in 1978, singer Carole King gave Satchidananda land in Connecticut that was sold to purchase more than 750 acres in Buckingham County. A tour of his land convinced him that this was the perfect location for the

LOTUS—Light Of Truth Universal Shrine, which was dedicated on July 20, 1986.

A lotus blossom-shaped temple might be the last thing you'd expect to find out in the Virginia countryside, but the building, with its large powder blue, soft pink, and pearly white petals, lends a calming beauty to its Blue Ridge Mountain surroundings. The form of the lotus blossom was chosen because it symbolizes the spiritual unfolding of the soul. Cool.

The LOTUS is a magnificent structure. The building is surrounded by fountains and pools. Satchidananda envisioned it as a place where people of all backgrounds and faiths could come together under one roof for silent meditation and contemplation. In keeping with that mission, the lower floor of the shrine contains artifacts and information on all major religions.

After your meditation in the LOTUS (sign up in the gift shop first), you can hike to the Lord Siva Nataraja Shrine on the hilltop above the LOTUS. This shrine is worth a visit to see the dancing statue of Lord Siva Nataraja, the King of Cosmic Dances. Wearing a flaming halo symbolizing the Pranava OM (universal intelligence/energy), the statue rotates for ten minutes every six hours—at noon, 6 p.m., midnight, and 6 a.m.

Oh, and don't forget to stop at the gift shop for a souvenir or two of your visit, such as a Hatha Yoga mug, an ergonomic meditation cushion, or a set of meditation flags.

The Chesapeake Bay Bridge Tunnel is the world's longest bridge-tunnel complex. Opened in 1964, it was immediately selected as one of the Seven Engineering Wonders of the Modern World. It carries US 13, and provides the only direct link between Virginia's Eastern Shore and Hampton Roads, Virginia.

Strange Theme Attractions

Dinosaur Kingdom • Natural Bridge

Shades of Jurassic Park! What if the Yankees had discovered a hidden valley of living dinosaurs and decided to use them as their secret weapons in the Civil War? Would these giant lizards eat up the Confederate Army in record time? Or ... would they defect and decide that blue uniforms make a much tastier treat?

At Dinosaur Kingdom, visitors are asked to imagine themselves in the year 1863. Imagine, then, that a family of Virginia paleontologists has discovered a hidden valley of dinosaurs. Unfortunately, the dastardly Union Army has learned of the discovery and has kidnapped the monsters to use against the Southern army.

Dinosaur Kingdom features Yankee soldiers being gobbled up by dinosaurs.
Photo by Mark Cline

Following the tour trail, you find just what folly this was, beginning with the angry, lunging, roaring T-Rex at the entrance. Continue, and you'll come upon scene upon scene of destruction and gore, with bluecoats being snatched up like Little Debbies at kindergarten snack time.

There are Yankees being eaten by snakes. Yankees being snatched from the back of a rearing horse by T-Rex. Yankees fighting off dinosaurs in trees. Even Yankees being attacked in the outhouse. Death and destruction everywhere.

Located on the property of Mark Cline's Haunted Monster Museum, Dinosaur Kingdom is a work in progress, with many more gory scenes planned. The giant fiberglass lizards, some with snapping jaws, mobile tongues, and sweeping tails, have been transplanted here from Glasgow, Virginia, where several years ago, Cline had placed them as a tourism draw. He billed Glasgow as The Town That Time Forgot. Guess time finally caught up with little Glasgow, and Cline was asked to remove the dinosaurs.

Located at Routes 130 and 11 at the Natural Bridge complex.

Dinosaur Land • White Post

Whoa! More giant lizards! Built in the mid-1960s, Dinosaur Land takes you back in time. No, not to prehistoric days. The kitschy park takes you back to a time when families loaded up in the trusty family station wagon and set out in search of sights to see. And there's plenty to be seen here.

No, the dinos don't have moving parts, but so what? They're big and they're ugly and they're everywhere. Scattered across the once barren expanse of land, you'll find every

B-movie monster you ever trembled to. Have your picture taken in the gentle hand of King Kong. Sit inside the mouth of a sixty-foot shark. Tangle with the seventy-foot octopus or pray with the fourteen-foot praying mantis.

And don't miss the dinosaurs. There are dinos fighting. Dinos laying eggs. Big dinos. Baby dinos. Dinos. Dinos. Dinos.

And, what sixties' roadside attraction would be complete without a souvenir shop? Here, you'll find everything from the tacky to the educational. It's kitschy fun that can't be missed.

Located at the intersection of U.S. 522 and Highway 340.

Haunted Monster Museum & Dark Maze • Natural Bridge

Another of Mark Cline's creations, the Haunted Monster Museum & Dark Maze tour begins as you walk through the open jaws of some giant cat-like creature that outlines the creepy, creaky gate. You light-foot it up a crumbling, long-abandoned asphalt driveway, through the Freaky Forest to the top of the hill, where stands the Haunted Monster Museum.

It's an abandoned 1870s stone Victorian house (a real one!), that Cline has embellished with his fiberglass creations, such as a giant skull and a python slithering in and out of the gables. With peeling paint and overgrown shrubbery, it's a spooky place, made more so by a sudden blast of dirge-like organ music.

You may find yourself trembling as you follow the instructions of a sign on a phone booth, dialing 13 to hear a hysterical voice warning you to get out before it's too late. But, of course, you have no intention of leaving, do you?

Located at the intersection of Routes 130 and 11 in the Natural Bridge complex.

Holy Land, USA • Bedford

Always wanted to visit the Holy Land, but were afraid of those suicide bombers? Well, in Bedford's Holy Land, USA, you can tour some of the Bible lands of Israel, Syria, and Jordan, and about the only thing you'd have to fear in this nature sanctuary would be a band of marauding raccoons.

The three-mile trail takes you on a journey through the life and deeds of Jesus Christ. You begin the journey—where else?—in Bethlehem. You travel north through the Judean countryside to Shepherd's Field, populated by sheep and goats. Moving on down Jericho Road, you reach Jericho and journey into the Jordan Valley through Nain, then on to Galilee. Rest a bit in Nazareth, where you can explore Joseph's carpenter shop and drink from Mary's well.

All along the way, as you cross the historic Jordan River, skirt around the Sea of Galilee to Capernaum, and trod into Jerusalem, you'll find displays of significant biblical places and events, such as the baptismal pool in the Jordan River, the three crosses on Calvary Hill, Jesus' empty tomb, and the discovery of the Dead Sea Scrolls.

Admission to the park is free, and there's no charge for an unguided walking tour. There is a charge for riding and guided tours, which must be scheduled in advance.

Located at 1060 Jericho Road.

Strange Museums

Virginia is steeped in history, as evidenced by the large number of museums throughout the state. But you won't find works by Picasso and Monet hanging here. Nah. We're much more interesting than that.

American Armored Foundation Tank Museum • Danville

What better way to kick off our Strange Museum section than with the AAF Tank Museum! It's chock-full of strange but true stuff! Tanks! Vintage uniforms! Disembodied heads wearing weird hats! Blood and guts! They've got it all.

The German Panzer MKIV tank is one of the many exhibits at the AAF Tank Musuem. Courtesy of AAF Tank Museum

The museum, which was originally located in Mattituck, New York, was founded in 1981 with the mission to "educate, collect, restore, preserve, and display as varied a collection of military tank and cavalry artifacts as possible, so that present and future generations will have a significant military history available for them to learn from and explore." Mission accomplished.

Billed as the world's most extensive collection of international tanks and cavalry artifacts, the museum boasts more than three hundred thirty-three thousand square feet containing fifteen thousand international tank and cavalry artifacts dating all the way back to 1509. You'll be mesmerized by all the military might, including tanks, machine guns, mortars, flame throwers, and rocket launchers.

Those exhibits are pretty cool, but there's more! The exhibits of vintage uniforms include a display of thirty-two international children's uniforms, making us wonder which countries are drafting kids. There's an exhibit of tank and artillery optical instruments, and how 'bout that Elvis, His Military Years exhibit, or the battle display showing a bloody, disemboweled soldier. Not to be missed!

Our favorite exhibit by far is the Headgear of the World display. Here you'll find more than seven hundred military hats and helmets modeled by some pretty creepy-looking mannequin heads. The hats are pretty funky. Makes you wonder why these guys weren't laughed off the battlefield.

Located at 3401 U.S. Highway 29B.

Drug Enforcement Administration Museum • Arlington

Got an interest in drugs? No, man, not doin' 'em! Doing away with them. That's the focus of the DEA's museum in Arlington. Started in 1976, when, during the country's bicentennial celebration, the federal government encouraged all agencies to develop exhibits highlighting their history, the museum records the history of drug enforcement in the U.S.

There are interactive kiosks, a mini theater, literature, and exhibits on the history of illegal drugs in America. The archive contains more than two thousand items, including exhibits from an old-fashioned drugstore, an illegal crack house, a sixties' head shop, and a circa 1800 opium den. There's also a collection of badges dating back to 1914, the date the DEA was formed, photographs, documents, and oral histories of individuals involved in battling drugs and drug trafficking.

In addition to recording the DEA's history, the museum strives to educate children and adults on the evils of drug addiction through a series of programs and exhibits. The DEA: Air, Land, and Sea exhibit shows how the DEA is fighting the drug war in the air, on the land, and on the sea. The exhibit includes a helicopter and a dragster that are examples of how the DEA is expanding its land enforcement. Hey, cool it, man. It's the fuzz.

Located at 700 Army Navy Drive.

George Washington Masonic Memorial • Alexandria

The cornerstone for the George Washington Masonic Memorial was laid in 1923, one year after the groundbreaking and 130 years after President George Washington helped lower the cornerstone of the U.S. Capitol. President Calvin Coolidge used the same silver trowel used by Washington on that long ago day to spread the cement on the Masonic memorial. President Herbert Hoover participated in its dedication on May 12, 1932.

The 333-foot memorial took ten years to build. Each column weighs sixty tons and is forty feet high. The second floor columns are placed directly above those on the first floor, and they bear the weight of the entire nine stories of the building.

The architecture of the building and its interior are Egyptian, reminiscent of the buildings of ancient Alexandria. Inside, you'll find a myriad of rooms to tour, all filled with Masonic artifacts and lore.

Step into Memorial Hall, the front room, and you'll be greeted by a seventeen-foot, seven-ton bronze statue of George Washington, the Charter Master of Alexandria Lodge No. 22. There is also a mural by renowned artist Allyn Cox, showing Washington, in full Masonic regalia, at the September 18, 1793, laying of the Capitol cornerstone.

Each room contains furniture and other relics used by Washington in the original lodge in Old Towne Alexandria, including his library chair, the silver trowel, and his bedchamber clock, which was stopped at 10:20 p.m., the time of his death on December 14, 1799.

Located at 101 Callahan Drive.

George Washington National Birthplace Monument • Pope's Creek

Nope, George Washington wasn't born in Mount Vernon, despite what most think. Our first president actually first laid his head in Pope's Creek, a little township just down the way from Mount Vernon. And, hey, guess what? You can see that house where such a hallowed first breath was taken. Well, sorta.

See, the original family home burned in 1779 and was not

rebuilt. The burn site was neglected for many years, and its exact location was lost. Then, in 1930 someone came up with an idea. Hey! We need a new historic site (read: tourist attraction). A memorial home, which may or may not resemble the original because no one remembers what the original looked like, was built on what may or may not be the original site. Actually, subsequent excavation of the land shows that the home is not built on the original site. Oh, well. They tried.

Today, the National Park Service operates a colonial farm here, complete with costumed interpreters who re-create the "sights, sounds, and smells of eighteenth-century plantation life." There are tours available daily that include the memorial house, the colonial kitchen, spinning shop, and farm buildings. There's also a museum, picnicking along Pope's Creek, and a one-mile nature hike. You can even visit the Washington family burial site, where George's father, grandfather, and great-grandfather are buried.

Located at 1732 Pope's Creek Road.

Jeane Dixon Museum and Library • Strasburg

Cue *Twilight Zone* music. This museum displays the personal items of Jeane Dixon, the psychic best known for predicting President John Kennedy's assassination. Seems that back in 1956, Dixon predicted in *Parade* magazine that the 1960 presidential election would be won by a Democrat who would be assassinated or would die in office. Of course, she also predicted that World War III would begin in 1958, a cure for cancer would be found in 1967, and that the Russians would be the first to land on the moon. Huh.

Jeane Dixon is best known as the psychic who predicted John F. Kennedy's assassination.
Courtesy of the Jeane Dixon Library and Museum

The Jeane Dixon Museum and Library is a collection of personal items and papers that seeks to interpret Dixon's life objectively. Her bedroom contains her elegant canopied bed, once owned by royalty, numerous gowns, hats, and religious icons. Scattered throughout the museum are works of art, mementos from Dixon's travels, and gifts from friends. The library contains hundreds of books on prophecy, some of which she wrote, studies on the paranormal, and books and magazines that featured her.

Located at 132 North Massanutten Street.

John Q. Adams Center for the History of Otolaryngology-Head and Neck Surgery • Alexandria

Whew! That's a mouthful. Get it? Mouthful? Head and neck? Never mind.

This museum is a bizarre collection of historical instruments used in head and neck surgery through the ages. Many of them, heck, most of them, resemble instruments of torture.

There's the three-pronged metal Chinese ear cleaning instrument, great for digging out that stubborn earwax; a set of tonsil screws (we didn't know they screwed in!); metal tracheotomy tubes; and a wild collection of hearing aids, including a really cool brass ear trumpet dating back to 1900.

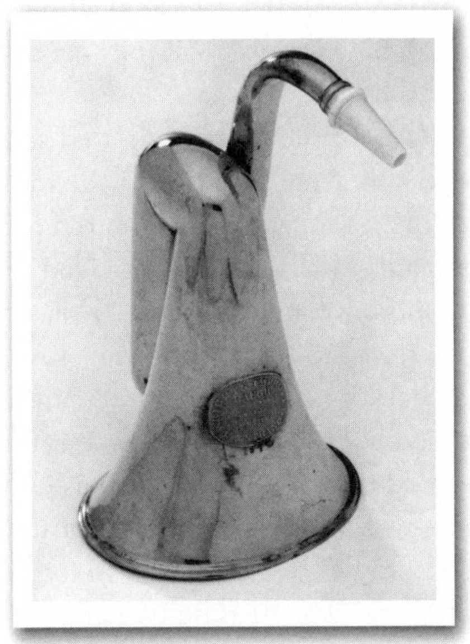

Most early ear trumpets, like this bugle-type c. 1900, were custom made.
Courtesy of the Adams Center, AAO-HNSF

Named in honor of John Q. Adams, founder of Adams Laboratories, the museum also chronicles the history of head and neck surgery through various collections of research, educational programs, and oral (ha!) histories. It's located within the American Academy of Otolaryngology-Head and Neck Surgery Foundation.

Located at One Prince Street.

MacArthur Museum • Norfolk

Douglas MacArthur spent his early years traveling the globe as an Army brat of Arthur MacArthur Jr., who climbed the ranks to general. After graduating West Point in 1903, Douglas began his own rise—all the way to Supreme Commander of the Allied Powers in Japan.

One of the most decorated soldiers in U.S. history, MacArthur was also one of the most controversial figures in history. He was greatly admired for his strategic and tactical brilliance, but was also criticized for his actions in command and his egotistical attitude. That egotistical attitude, in fact, may have led to his dismissal.

Back in 1950, when the Chinese People's Liberation Army forced U.N. troops to retreat at the Yalu River, MacArthur wanted to use nuclear weapons on the Chinese—as many as fifty, he said. President Harry Truman knew a nuclear strike might draw the Soviet Union into the struggle, thereby setting off World War III. The two argued heatedly, and on April 11, 1951, Truman—who was Supreme Commander of All—relieved MacArthur of duty.

In his farewell address to Congress, MacArthur said "Old soldiers never die. They just fade away." That's just what the ol' man did. He spent the rest of his life quietly in New York until his death in 1964.

MacArthur and his wife, Jean, are buried together in a monumental rotunda in downtown Norfolk. The rotunda is festooned with banners, flags, and inscriptions about MacArthur's illustrious military career. Nine separate galleries on two levels circle the rotunda and tell the story of MacArthur and the millions of soldiers who served in the military from the Civil War through the Korean War.

The beautifully landscaped MacArthur Square, erected around the rotunda, is the site of four buildings comprising the MacArthur Memorial. The memorial's theater contains special exhibit galleries and continuously shows a film on the life of the general. The Jean MacArthur Research Center houses the library, archives, and educational programs.

A museum located within Norfolk's nineteenth-century City Hall houses personal artifacts and memorabilia, including medals, flags, paintings, weapons, and military equipment. The gift shop also houses MacArthur's 1950 Chrysler Imperial limousine.

Located downtown on MacArthur Square.

Mariner's Museum • Newport News

Ahoy, matie! Here's everything you ever wanted to know about the history of man and the sea. Considered one of the finest maritime museums in the country, the Mariner's Museum encompasses more than sixty thousand square feet of gallery space, filled with all things nautical.

The model exhibit contains more than fifteen hundred intricately carved ship models, documenting every type of vessel ever constructed, from a Chinese Sampan to a huge model of the Queen Elizabeth II. Many are creations of world-renowned model makers August and Winifred Crabtree.

The museum's most celebrated exhibition is that of the USS *Monitor*, the ironclad ship sunk during the Civil War. The wreck was discovered in 1973, and since that time, efforts have been made to recover and conserve as much of it as possible.

The Maritime Museum currently displays items such as the ship's anchor, silverware, badges, lanterns, and ceramic pieces.

The exhibit's most popular piece, of course, is the ship's revolving gun turret, which is on limited display until completion of the USS *Monitor* Center, scheduled for March 2007. The $30 million center will house a full scale replica of the USS *Monitor*.

Handcrafted by August F. Crabtree, this ship is part of an exhibit documenting the evolution of the sailing ship.
Courtesy of The Mariner's Museum

It's a good idea to bring your lunch when you visit the Maritime Museum. Not only will you spend hours exploring the many exhibits, but you'll also want to explore the museum's 550 wooded acres, complete with a five-mile trail around Lake Maury, hiking, and picnicking.

Located at 100 Museum Drive.

MONTICELLO • CHARLOTTESVILLE

If his home is any indication, Thomas Jefferson was a man who couldn't be satisfied. He spent forty years of his life designing, building, tearing apart, redesigning, and rebuilding it. The more than five hundred thousand bricks used in various constructions of Monticello were baked in kilns on the grounds.

The home and its construction were never far from his thoughts, even when he was away—serving as minister to France and later as U.S. president. While in France, he filled almost one hundred crates with furniture, artwork, and fruit trees. During his presidency, he would make the trip home whenever possible. It was his wish to die here.

Built on a mountain, Monticello, which means "little mountain" in Italian, was meant to be a working plantation, but though Jefferson was able to eke out enough to feed and clothe his family, the plantation did not produce enough money to support the country gentleman lifestyle he preferred. That necessitated drastic measures.

It's a cruel irony that the man who wrote the Declaration of Independence, the very document that declared all men equal, utilized slavery on his plantation in order to support himself in a rich lifestyle. He often said he deplored slavery, and owned slaves simply because he needed the money. Guess it was a case of "do as I say, not as I do."

Despite this considerable flaw, Jefferson was a great man who spent forty years in public service. He died—at Monticello—on July 4, 1826, an ironic date, since July 4 was the date Congress accepted the final draft of the Declaration of Independence.

After Jefferson's death, practically everything was sold to settle his debts (guess that slave labor didn't help out all that much), but in the last seventy years, the Thomas Jefferson

Memorial Foundation has worked to reacquire the home and as many of Jefferson's possessions as possible.

Today, you can tour Monticello and its beautifully landscaped grounds. Some of the items that have been recovered and are on display include Native American artifacts presented to Jefferson by Lewis and Clark; an astronomical clock he built because the less accurate clocks of the day made him miss the eclipse of 1811; his original dining room tables; and more than thirty paintings.

Located at 931 Thomas Jefferson Parkway.

Mount Vernon • Mount Vernon

Mount Vernon was George Washington's home for more than forty-five years. The estate, first known as Little Hunting Creek Plantation, was originally granted to Washington's great-grandfather in 1674. Washington inherited it from his older half-brother, who had renamed it Mount Vernon after his commanding officer, Admiral Edward Vernon of the British Navy.

When Washington first acquired the plantation, it was small. Though the family home was called the Mansion House Farm, it was far from mansion-sized, with just four rooms downstairs and three upstairs. There were just two thousand acres of land to be farmed.

Washington immediately set about enlarging and improving the plantation, adding six thousand more acres and expanding the house to twenty-one rooms. A beautiful two-story piazza, paved with white English flagstones, was added in 1777. It was a favorite warm weather gathering spot for family and friends.

One of the last touches Washington added was a cupola, which not only was a decorative rooftop touch, but also provided cooling in hot weather. Washington's final touch was the white dove of peace weathervane atop the cupola.

The Mount Vernon Ladies' Association purchased Mount Vernon from the Washington family in 1858 and restored it to its 1799 condition, the year Washington died. It was opened to the public in 1860, and more than eighty million visitors have toured the estate.

George Washington lived at Mount Vernon for more than forty-five years.
Courtesy of VTC

Located at 3200 Mount Vernon Memorial Highway.

National Museum of the Civil War Soldier • Petersburg

This is more than a museum. It's an adventure. Forget walking around and looking at ol' stuff. In this museum, you get an up-close and personal view of the life of a Civil War soldier.

Upon entering, you're assigned a personal Civil War soldier to guide you through the seven-gallery exhibit, titled Duty Called Me Here. Using interactive computers, videos, MP3 players, life-size dioramas, and more than one thousand original artifacts, you learn all about your soldier's life, from his religion, to diseases he may have suffered, to the hardships of war.

The tour culminates with Trial by Fire, a "multi-sensory" battlefield simulation. You'll experience the sights, sounds, and even the feel of battle, with cannon explosions rattling your teeth and the sound of musket fire surrounding you. You'll leave wild-eyed and trembling.

The National Museum of the Civil War Soldier offers high-tech features in addition to a large selection of Civil War uniforms and artifacts throughout eight galleries.
Courtesy of Pamplin Historical Park

But pull yourself together. There's more to see in the twenty-five thousand-square-foot museum. There's the Remembrance Wall, a mahogany wall with silver plaques etched with the name and company of Civil War soldiers. Have a relative who served, but don't see his name? For a small fee, you can have that name—along with yours—added to the wall.

The Civil War Store is the place to buy all sorts of historical items, including Civil War clothing, art, jewelry, videos, limited-edition collectibles, and books. If all that battling made you hungry, be sure to stop by the Hard Tack and Coffee Café for a bite before you leave.

The National Museum of the Civil War Soldier, located within Pamplin Historical Park, has won numerous national and international awards. It's considered one of the best museums in the country.

Located at 6125 Boydton Plank Road.

THE OLD COAST GUARD STATION • VIRGINIA BEACH

Didn't see enough seafaring stuff at the Maritime Museum? Well, don't despair. There's more. The Old Coast Guard Station, built in 1903 as a Life-Saving/Coast Guard Station in Virginia Beach, has been preserved and now houses two floors of collections and exhibits of the Coast Guard in action.

The Lower Gallery, which was once the boat room, tells the story of the Life-Saving Service, with exhibits showing rescue equipment and methods. The Upper Gallery is where the lifeguards, called surfmen (bet Pamela Anderson's not too pleased with that chauvinistic title), slept. Today, it houses tales of Virginia shipwrecks and the Battle of the Atlantic in World War II.

Still not enough? Well, get involved in the Old Coast Guard Station's Shipwreck Identification Project. This is an ongoing project designed to discover and preserve wooden shipwrecks that occasionally wash up on shore following storms.
Just such a wreck was found following Hurricane Isabel in October 2003, when a local citizen stumbled upon it. Preliminary research suggests the wreck was a cargo schooner

from the late nineteenth century. It was at least one hundred feet in length. The museum plans to place portions of the ship in an exhibit on the museum grounds.

Located at 24th Street and Boardwalk.

Oyster and Maritime Museum • Chincoteague

When the Oyster Museum opened in 1972, it was the only museum in the country dedicated to the oyster. Imagine that. Must've been difficult drawing in tourists just offering a look at a slimy little bottom feeder, though, because in recent years the museum has expanded to include a variety of marine exhibits. The name has even been changed. It's now the Oyster and Maritime Museum.

The museum chronicles the story of the oyster and the seafood business, a major industry in Chincoteague. There are exhibits of oyster farming implements—many of them turn-of-the-century. And you certainly won't want to miss the oystering diorama, complete with scows on the water, harvesting methods, and the shucking process!

In addition, there's an aquarium, marine exhibits, such as the Fresnel lens from the Assateague Lighthouse, a library that chronicles the history of the island, and a museum store.

Located at 7125 Maddox Boulevard.

Peanut Museum • Waverly

Well, here's a nutty museum, or at least it would be if the peanut were really a nut. But it's not. It's a legume—like a pea. Get it? Pea-nut? Bet you didn't know that.

Anyhoo, the country's first ever peanut museum is located in Waverly, a fitting home since Waverly is the site of Virginia's first commercial peanut crop. Seems that back in the 1830s, Dr. Matthew Harris of Waverly obtained a few peanuts and planted them. He experimented with them for several years. Then in 1842, he sold his first batch commercially in the streets of Petersburg.

The peanut didn't become a major agricultural crop in Virginia until the 1900s, when the boll weevil ate its way through the South's cotton crop. Today, peanuts are a multimillion dollar business in Virginia, with up to one hundred million pounds—3 percent of the nation's production—produced annually.

The Peanut Museum is located inside the Miles B. Carpenter Museum, an 1890 Victorian house that contains three museums. You'll learn everything you never wanted to know about the lowly peanut here. There are photographs, antique peanut tools, even peanut critters!

And if looking at all that peanut memorabilia makes you hungry for the salty little snack, just mosey on down the road a bit to Wakefield, where you'll find the Virginia Diner, which bills itself as The Peanut Capital of the World. It offers complimentary buckets of roasted peanuts, and their famous peanut pie!

Still not enough? Stroll across the street to the Plantation Peanuts of Virginia store. It's the building with the antique peanut digger in front. Here you'll find peanut products, and learn about all the ways to store, prepare, and cook peanuts.

Located near the intersection of Route 460 and Route 40.

PEST HOUSE MUSEUM • LYNCHBURG

Pestilence. Death. Medical instruments of torture. And it's all located in a cemetery. Now this is our kind of museum!

The Pest House, aka House of Pestilence Museum, was Lynchburg's first hospital, built in the 1840s. It was located at the outer edge of town and next to the Public Burying Ground (City Cemetery) for good reason. Those confined here were infected with an infectious disease—smallpox, cholera, or scarlet fever. You wanted to keep them as far away from the uninfected as possible, and, standards of cleanliness being what they were, having a cemetery close by was quite convenient.

The Pest House was Lynchburg's first hospital.
Courtesy of Southern Memorial Association/Old City Cemetery

By 1862, Lynchburg had become a major Civil War hospital center, and the Pest House was used as the quarantine hospital for Confederate soldiers. It was run by Dr. John Terrell, a thirty-three-year-old physician, who knew a thing or two about infection control. The control methods he introduced reduced the mortality rate from 50 percent to 5 percent. After the war, Terrell opened an office near his home, from which he practiced for many years.

The original Pest House building was lost, but in 1987, the Southern Medical Association moved Dr. Terrell's office building to the City Cemetery and restored it as the House of

Peanuts! Get your hot roasted peanuts! Imagine attending a ball game and not hearing that cry. Imagine no peanut butter sandwich. No roadside stands offering hot boiled peanuts.

The fact is that the peanut is a relatively new crop to North America. The plant is believed to have originated in Brazil or Peru, because thirty-five hundred year-old pottery jars shaped like peanuts have been discovered there. Peanuts were grown in Mexico by the time the Spanish arrived. The Spanish took them back to Spain, where they are still grown. From there, they were disseminated to Asia and Africa, where they were regarded as one of several plants to possess a soul.

The peanut finally arrived in America in the 1700s, along with the African slaves. The nickname "goober" stems from "nguba," the African word for peanut. Back in those days, the peanut, known then as the ground pea or ground nut, was considered food for the poor. It was also considered an excellent food for pigs.

Commercial production was inhibited because of the difficulty in harvesting until the 1900s, when labor-saving machinery made things easier. Then, that pesky boll weevil struck, and the rest is peanut history.

Pestilence Museum. Here, you'll find a re-creation of the wretched conditions of the original Pest House. You'll also find original furnishings and medical equipment used by Terrell, including his operating table, an 1860s hypodermic needle, an "asthma chair," a "poison chest" (drug box), and, best of all, a pre-1885 surgical amputation kit. Cool!

Located at 401 Taylor Street.

Railroad Museums • Crewe/ Parksley/ Fairfax/ Roanoke/ Richmond

The railroad played a huge role in Virginia's development. As a result, you'll find railroad museums scattered across the state. Here's a sample.

The Crewe Railroad Museum in Crewe is located adjacent to the Norfolk Southern Railroad tracks. It houses memorabilia from the Norfolk & Western and other railroads. The museum has a diesel engine, coal car, two boxcars, and a caboose. The diesel and caboose are open to the public. Located on U.S. Highway 460.

The Eastern Shore Railway Museum, located within a train depot, has a model train exhibit, antique railcars, and railroad memorabilia. An 1890s maintenance shed contains antique tools and other railway artifacts. Located at 18468 Dunne Avenue, Parksley.

The Fairfax Station Railroad Museum houses Civil War, Red Cross, and historic railway artifacts. Located in Fairfax Station at 11200 Fairfax Station Road.

The O. Winston Link Museum houses galleries of O.

Winston Link's 1950s photographs. Link was a photographer who had a penchant for photographing trains, particularly Norfolk & Western trains, and the people who operated them and rode on them. In his quest to capture the best photo, he experimented with lighting and shutter techniques. The museum is located in the restored Norfolk & Western passenger station, and features more than 250 of Link's railway photographs, along with interactive exhibits and train viewing areas. Located at 101 Shenandoah Avenue, Roanoke.

The Old Dominion Railway Museum contains historic passenger coaches and engines for use on excursion rides. The museum is housed within an express car of the Richmond, Fredericksburg, and Potomac Railroad Company. Located at 102 Hull Street, Richmond.

SCIENCE MUSEUM OF VIRGINIA • RICHMOND

Even if you weren't good in science at school, you'll enjoy a visit to the Science Museum. Located within the renovated Broad Street Railroad Station, the museum is filled to the brim with exciting interactive exhibits that let you learn as you do.

You'll learn all about astronomy, DNA, crime fighting with forensics, and how gems are

The Grand Kugel, a twenty-nine-ton, eight-foot, eight-inch diameter granite globe, floats in front of the Science Museum of Virginia.
Courtesy of the Science Museum of Virginia

formed. Play laser pool and watch a special pendulum prove that the Earth does, indeed, rotate. There's also space exploration, dinosaur fossils, plus sparking electricity exhibits, and snakes, frogs, and spiders. An IMAX theater features a wide variety of planetarium shows.

Located at 2500 West Broad Street. You can't miss it. It's the building with a huge black globe in front.

STEVEN F. UDVAR-HAZY CENTER • CHANTILLY

When you and I run out of space, we hold a garage sale. Where, though, would you sell a 174,750-pound jet? That was the dilemma facing the Smithsonian Institute's National Air and Space Museum in Washington, D.C. So, what did they do? What else? They built more space.

The Steven F. Udvar-Hazy Center, named for the guy who shelled out the most cash, opened on December 15, 2003—just days away from the one hundreth anniversary of the Wright brother's first flight—displaying hundreds of airships.

The center's Aviation Hangar is ten stories high and the length of three football fields. The John S. McDonnell Hangar is a bit smaller, but not much. The hangars contain 119 aircraft, 142 large space artifacts, and more than fifteen hundred smaller items.

Among the many displays in the Aviation Hangar, you'll find the Lockheed SR-71 Blackbird, the fastest jet in the world, Warhawks, Phantoms, and Hellcats. The Enola Gay, the plane that dropped the first atomic bomb on Hiroshima, is there. You'll also find small planes, helicopters, and ultralights.

Located at 14390 Air and Space Museum Parkway.

Tobacco Farm Life Museum • South Hill

Tobacco is gold in South Hill. Incorporated in 1901, the town has always been known for its tobacco industry, and it is presently the third largest market in Virginia. No wonder, then, that there is a Tobacco Museum located here. Run by Pat Farrer, who grew up on a tobacco farm, the museum focuses on the lifestyle and activities of an early 1900s tobacco farm. You'll learn all about the production of tobacco, from seed to market. There's an authentic strip room (where the tobacco leaves strip, we assume, not big busted ladies) and a hand-cut log barn.

Located at 306 West Main Street.

Toy Museum • Natural Bridge

Still just a kid at heart? Then visit the Toy Museum, which boasts the largest collection of childhood memorabilia in the world. Miss that Barbie doll your stinky little brother decapitated way back when? You'll find one just like it here. How about you, stinky little brother? Wish you still had that G.I. Joe your sister flushed in retaliation for the Barbie doll stunt? No problem.

In the more than forty-five thousand museum items, you'll find both antique and modern collectible dolls, including the original Barbie, Ginny, Shirley Temple, and Madame Alexander series. There's also a pair of dolls, the oldest museum artifacts, that were made in 1740 and were displayed in Savannah, Virginia, during the American Revolution.

There are action figures galore, including first edition G.I. Joes, Masters of the Universe, Teenage Mutant Ninja Turtles, and many more. There are *Star Trek*, *Star Wars*, and *Planet of the Apes* figures, robots, play sets, mechanical toys, train sets, and

Virginia Tobacco Facts

1. Tobacco is Virginia's largest cash crop.
2. Virginia is the fourth largest tobacco producing state in the country.
3. Virginia is the country's second largest tobacco manufacturing state.
4. There are four types of tobacco grown in Virginia: burley, flue-cured, fire-cured, and sun-cured.
5. The ports of Hampton Roads are the nation's largest ports exporting tobacco and tobacco products.
6. Tobacco production began in Virginia when John Rolfe acquired seed from the Spanish colonies. The first shipments of Virginia-grown tobacco reached England in 1614.
7. Flue-cured tobacco is most often called "flue-cured Virginia," because Virginia was the first state to use an artificial heat method of curing.
8. Flue-cured Virginia is now produced in many nations around the world, including Australia, Canada, Africa, and South America.
9. The Philip-Morris Manufacturing Center in Richmond is the country's largest cigarette plant. It processes 1.2 million pounds of tobacco daily.

your favorite games, including that best one called Cooties. Oh! Oh! And don't miss the Mr. Potato Head! Wasn't he such fun! This just might be the bestest place in the world!

Located on Route 11.

USS Wisconsin • Norfolk

The *Wisky*, as it's affectionately known by Norfolk residents, was launched on December 3, 1943, and served bravely throughout WWII, the Korean War, and even as recently as Desert Storm. She was finally mothballed in 2000 and is now permanently berthed in Norfolk.

The USS *Wisconsin* sits in port at Nauticus.
Photo by Dom Menta

The ship's nickname is not a shortening of her name, but rather stems from a 1956 accident. On May 6, 1956, while cruising in a dense fog off the Virginia Capes, the *Wisconsin* collided with the destroyer USS *Eaton*, causing severe damage to her bow. She was placed into dry dock at the Norfolk Naval Shipyard, where a 120-ton, sixty-eight-foot section of the uncompleted battleship *Kentucky* was used to repair the damage. Get it? Wis…KY.

Tours of the ship are available through the Hampton Roads Naval Museum. The tours are free and are self-guided, though docents are present throughout the ship to answer questions. The docents are supremely knowledgeable about all areas of the ship. They should be. They're all retired sailors who once served there. The tour covers only the exterior areas of the ship. The interior is locked because, despite her age, the *Wisky* could be recalled into service in the case of a national emergency.

The museum is located at One Waterside Drive.

Virginia Museum of Transportation • Roanoke

The Virginia Museum of Transportation is home to a large collection of vintage land transportation vehicles. Guys will just go nuts over the automobiles, which include a 1920 Buick Touring Car, a 1924 Ford Model T, and a 1930 Chevrolet Stake Bed Truck.

There's also something for you soccer moms—the very first station wagon! Seems that back in the 1800s, a designer came up with the plans for a vehicle resembling a motorized stagecoach, which was manufactured

The Virginia Museum of Transportation houses vintage land transportation vehicles.
Courtesy of Roanoke CVB/VTC

in Jamaica. The design was popular, and he was the only one who was selling them. So, when folks asked where they were made, wanting to hold that exclusivity, the designer replied "Rockaway." The car became known as the Rockaway, and was called that even after the cat was let out of the bag, and the car was being sold by every Tom, Dick, and Harry around. Somewhere around 1890, however, someone came up with a new name for the popular carriage, and it became known as the station wagon.

The museum also has a large number of vintage trains for viewing, some of them the only one of its kind left. Big and little boys alike, and even some of us tomboys, will love the multilevel electric train set that has viewing levels for all sizes.

Located at 303 Norfolk Avenue.

Virginia War Museum • Newport News

War! Huh! What is it good for! Absolutely...Well, maybe it does make for an interesting museum.

American military history from 1775 to the 1970s unfolds at the Virginia War Museum. The American Revolution. The War of 1812. The Mexican War. The Civil War. The Indian Wars. World War I. World War II. The Korean War. The Vietnam War. That's a lot of warring, and you'll find lots of war stuff in the America and War exhibit. You'll find everything from uniforms to weapons to artwork to one of the first battle tanks ever made.

The Women at War exhibit examines the changing role of women in war, including Red Cross workers, nurses, and members of the military. The March to Freedom exhibit honors the contributions of African-Americans in the military, from the

Revolutionary War to the Gulf War, and examines the parallels between the history of African-Americans in the military and the struggle for civil rights. Other exhibits include such items as a section of the Berlin Wall and a portion of a wall from the Dachau Concentration Camp.

Located at 9285 Warwick Boulevard.

Walton Mountain Museum • Schuyler

Good night, Ben. Good night, Mary Ellen. Good night, Mama. Good night, Daddy. If you listen hard enough, you might just hear those saccharin last words from the television series *The Waltons* echoing around the Blue Ridge Mountains. Well, maybe only in your imagination, since the show was actually filmed in California.

But if the show rang Blue Ridge Mountain true, it's because its creator and narrator, Earl Hamner Jr., grew up in these mountains during the Great Depression. His mountain home of Schuyler, population four hundred, is as close to Walton Mountain as you could possibly get. The characters of the show were based on his large family, which included his seven brothers and sisters. John Boy, the lead character, was based on ol' Earl himself, who was, indeed, the writer of the family.

You can learn all about Hamner and the Waltons at the Walton Mountain Museum, located in the old elementary school from which Hamner graduated in 1940. The guided tours take you through several rooms replicating the show set, starting out in the kitchen containing a replica of the famous Walton table and Depression-era antiques.

The living room is filled with 1930s furniture, similar to that used on the Walton's set. There's even the actual radio used in the show! John Boy's room, of course, has a bed, a chest, and his ol' Underwood typewriter sitting on a desk. There's also a case that blends John Boy's life with Earl's, including his two Emmys and the horn from the Walton's truck. In the Recipe Room, you'll find the Baldwin Sisters' recipe for moonshine, a moonshine still, and a comprehensive history on moonshine making.

There's even a Godsey's Store (and Gift Shop), though you'll find items here that you'd never find on Walton Mountain, such as show videos, Beanie Babies, and Walton's calendars.

Good night, John Boy.

Located on Route 617.

The Newseum, the world's first interactive museum of news, opened in Arlington, Virginia, in 1997 to celebrate "the value of a unique American notion—the First Amendment." Administrative offices remain in Arlington while the facility prepares for a move to Washington, D.C., in 2007.

The Haunting of Virginia

Mist rising on moonlit nights. Ghostly apparitions floating through hallowed halls. Strange and scary noises. Virginia can be a spooky place at night. Here's just a smattering of Virginia's legendary ghost tales.

APPOMATTOX MANOR • HOPEWELL

At different times during the Civil War, Appomattox Manor, built in 1635, served as a place to hole up for both Confederate and Union soldiers. From June 1864 until April 1865, it served as the official headquarters for General Ulysses S. Grant.

A legend surrounding the house holds that an unnamed nurse was tending to a Union soldier in the house when a Confederate troop rode up. She hid the soldier behind a wall in the basement, hoping to get rid of the Rebs and return to him. Unfortunately, in her haste, she forgot about the soldier's uniform and weapons. When the Confederates discovered them, the woman was arrested and taken away. The soldier, unable to free himself from the wall, died there.

Today, visitors to Appomattox Manor often report the sound of tapping and scratching on the walls. The story gains credibility when you learn that when the house was rebuilt in 1953, the skeleton of a Union soldier was found behind a wall in the basement.

Located on Cedar Lane.

BARTER THEATRE • ABINGDON

This theatre was founded by Robert Porterfield, who brought unemployed actors from New York to start the theatre during the Great Depression. Porterfield died in 1971, but his spirit still haunts the place. Actors have claimed to see him sitting in the audience, as he often did when he was alive.

Barter Theatre is haunted by its founder, Robert Porterfield.
Courtesy of VTC

Porterfield's ghost seems to be a benevolent spirit. Not so of the theatre's other ghost. He's said to be quite malevolent, often chasing actors from their dressing rooms.

Located at 127 West Main Street.

BUNNYMAN BRIDGE • CLIFTON

This may well be the most famous haunted place in Virginia. It has been featured on television and the Internet, and was named one of the Scariest Places on Earth by the Fox Family Channel in 2001.

It seems that in 1904, a bus transporting insane asylum inmates to the Lorton Prison crashed on the bridge. All but one were recaptured. Seems that this guy, quite insane, began hanging people from the bridge. When authorities looked for him underneath the bridge, they found a mass grave of little bunny carcasses—hence the bridge's name. The crazy man's spirit is said to haunt the bridge, and sometimes ghostly apparitions of bodies hanging from the bridge can be seen.

Danville Museum of Fine Arts and History • Danville

This museum is located within the historic Sutherlin Mansion, which was the home of Major William Sutherlin, wartime quartermaster for Danville. For the week of April 3-10, 1865, the major opened his home to Jefferson Davis and the Confederate government. It was here that Davis wrote and delivered his final proclamation to the Confederacy on April 4, and later met with his Cabinet for the last time. Because of that, the home and Danville have become known as the Last Capital of the Confederacy.

With such heavy events occurring here, it's no wonder that the place is haunted. It was said that Davis spent hours staring out the window of his upstairs bedroom, contemplating, no doubt, his surrender to the Union. At night, it's said that you can hear heavy footsteps pacing and smell cigar smoke.

Located at 975 Main Street.

George Mason University • Fairfax

The campus of this college has a couple of discombobulated spirits running around.

One is that of a young man who supposedly drowned in the campus lake. The next morning, his body was found sitting in a nearby gazebo. Today, there are reports of the young man wandering in the area around the gazebo. Often, he can be seen sitting in the gazebo, beckoning for young women to come sit beside him. Seems he's a bit shy, though, for if a woman does sit down next to him, he disappears.

The other George Mason ghost is known as Old Man Johnson, who lived in the area in the 1970s and often rowed on the lake where the George Mason crew team practices. The story goes that poor Old Man Johnson came home one day to find his wife in bed with another man. So what does he do? Right, he jumps in his trusty boat and rows over the Occoquan River dam, never to be seen again—well, alive that is. Members of the George Mason crew team have reported seeing his ghost in the early morning mists near the dam. It's become so common that whenever something strange happens at the college, it's said to be the work of Old Man Johnson.

Located at 4400 University Drive.

GOVERNOR'S PALACE • WILLIAMSBURG

Cool! The Williamsburg governor gets to live in a palace! And it's haunted, no less. Rumor has it that the palace and the palace green are haunted by the ghost of young Elizabeth, who was attending a ball at the governor's palace. For reasons unspecified, Elizabeth became upset and ran from the ballroom, leaving a shoe on the palace green. Now, why does that sound familiar...?

Anyhoo ... in one version of the story, upon returning home, Elizabeth threw herself off the top step (must've been a pretty high step) and died. Another version has her leaving

Williamsburg in shame and dying in childbirth. Whatever. Now she haunts the palace and the green. Since her footsteps are those of someone missing a shoe, we can only guess that she's come back to retrieve it. Must've been a Manolo Blahnik.

Located appropriately on Palace Street.

The ghost of the Governor's Palace, Elizabeth, is looking for her lost shoe.
Photo by Douglas Peebles/Courtesy of VTC

HOLLINS UNIVERSITY • ROANOKE

Hollins University is quite haunted. The hauntings have been a focus

Virginia ranks at the top of the Haunted Places list of National Register of Haunted Locations (who knew there was one!), with more than seventy sites claiming to be haunted.

Many towns offer tours of their haunted places. The Ghosts of Williamsburg, the Ghosts of Yorktown, and the Ghosts of Charles City are just three of the numerous tours available. You'll be guided from place to place by candlelight, learning the history of the sites and of their resident ghosts.

of student research. In Presser Hall, doors shut by themselves and students find themselves locked in a practice room, only to have the door open easily minutes later.

In Presser Hall at Hollins University, doors shut by themselves.
Photo by Richard Boyd

Starkie House, which was once the Old Infirmary, is haunted by a ghost nurse dressed in old-fashioned clothing who visits students during the night. She feels their foreheads for fever and reportedly watches over them.

Hollins University is located at 7916 Williamson Road.

Martha Washington Inn • Abingdon

This inn is a popular hotel with visitors to Abingdon looking to take advantage of its AAA Four-Diamond rating. It's also pretty popular with folks looking to get the pants scared off them.

The inn has experienced many incarnations. Built in 1832 as a private residence, it has served as a finishing school for young ladies, a Civil War hospital, and a college.

With such a storied past, it's no wonder the place is

haunted. Seems that a plethora of spirits roams the halls, and the sightings are readily acknowledged by workers, who say they've been touched and pushed by unseen spirits. The management has even tried to cash in on the resident ghosts, briefly charging extra for a stay in Room 403.

See, that's the room haunted by Beth. It's speculated that Beth must've visited the site when it was a Civil War hospital, searching for her lover, a Yankee officer, who had been killed. Reportedly, she pined away (lot of that going around in those days!), dying a year later.

Martha Washington Inn is haunted by a riderless horse.
Photo by Keith Lanpher/ Courtesy of VTC

Humans aren't the only ghosts roaming around Martha Washington Inn. There have been numerous sightings of a riderless horse in search of his slain Union officer. Beth's love, perhaps? If so, he must've been a heck of a guy, seeing how both his horse and his girlfriend are still searching for him!

In addition to these ghosts, inn workers report recurring bloodstains. The story goes that a Confederate spy died on that particular spot, and no matter how many times the carpet is replaced, his bloodstains reappear.

Located at 150 West Main Street.

MONTICELLO • CHARLOTTESVILLE

Thomas Jefferson so loved his mountainside home that it's easy to believe he would not want to leave it even in death. Couple that with the fact that he died here, and it's a safe bet that he still wanders the grounds. Monticello employees often report hearing him whistling, as he was known to do.

Thomas Jefferson spent many years remodeling Monticello.
Photo by Keith Lanpher/Courtesy of VTC

There have also been sightings of a young boy wearing a uniform and a tri-cornered hat. He was seen peering out of a second story window. Employees disavow any knowledge of him.

Located at 931 Thomas Jefferson Parkway.

PATRICK HENRY HOTEL • ROANOKE

This National Historic Landmark has more than just history to entertain you during your stay here. You can also get the bejesus scared outta you by the resident haints. The elegant hotel is home to the apparitions of three men who have been seen walking the halls and watching people dance in the ballroom.

It's also apparently the former home of Miss Lucy, who roams the halls of the hotel, which once housed her apartment. There have been more than forty reports of guests and staff members seeing a lady in a long white dress. One flight attendant, who had requested to stay in Miss Lucy's room, fled after seeing a stairway come out of the wall and a lady walk down it and across the room.

Located at 617 South Jefferson Street.

Ramsey House • Alexandria

The Ramsey House, built in 1724, is a National Historic Landmark. It also serves as the Alexandria Visitor's Center and is a stop on Alexandria's ghost tour, so visiting this haunted site should be no problem. The house is said to be haunted by John Carlyle, Alexandria's founder, and by sundry other spirits dressed in 1700s attire.

Located at 221 King Street.

Sherwood Forest Plantation • Charles City

One stop on Charles City's haunted tour, the Sherwood Forest Plantation was the home of President John Tyler from 1842 until his death in 1862. Built in 1720, the mansion has been the continuous residence of the family since Tyler bought it in 1842. It's also home to the Gray Lady, one of Virginia's most famous ghosts, thanks to L.B. Taylor Jr. and his book *Ghosts of Williamsburg*.

Sherwood Forest's present owners believe that the Gray Lady has been around since at least the eighteenth century, and, yes, they have encountered her several times in their years there. Their encounters are eerily similar to the reports handed down through the ages.

Because in sightings of the spirit lady she's always wearing gray—the color of servants' uniforms at Sherwood Forest—it is believed that she was a nanny at the plantation at some point. In these encounters, the spirit walks up the plantation's hidden stairway to a second-floor room, assumed to be a former nursery. Her distinct footsteps can be heard ascending the stairs, and then the sound of a rocking chair rocking in the upstairs room can be heard. There's further speculation that the child in her care died, and that's the reason the nanny has returned to the house after death.

Sherwood Forest Plantation was the home of the tenth president, John Tyler.
Courtesy of Sherwood Forest Plantation/Williamsburg Area CVB

There have been many instances where the owners and guests have experienced an encounter with the lady, either hearing her footsteps up and down the stairway, or in some instances, even closer, walking through their own rooms.

Payne Tyler, the present mistress of the house, isn't so sure that the Gray Lady was once a nanny, however. Intrigued by her encounters, she invited two psychics to visit. The first psychic reported seeing a tiny lady wearing an off-color dress, apron, and black shoes standing at the top of the stairs. The apparition disappeared when the psychic climbed the stairs.

It was the second psychic, though, that put the nanny theory in doubt. She also reported seeing a tiny lady dressed in a neutral-colored dress, apron, and black shoes. She followed the spirit into a bedroom and observed her folding clothes in front of a wardrobe, which she vividly described. It was an Empire wardrobe, dark brown, with a wide flange at the center, a large brass strip, and the design of dolphins at each foot.

Tyler was amazed. That very chest had been removed from the room two years earlier. It had been owned by John Tyler's wife, Julia, who loved dolphins. The chest had never been mentioned in literature about the house and had never been photographed. So, now, Tyler suspects that the ghost might, indeed, be a former mistress of the house—and First Lady.

Sherwood Forest is a National Historic Landmark. The grounds are open for tours daily. Located at 5416 Tuckahoe Avenue.

Shirley Plantation • Charles City

Built in 1613, the Shirley Plantation is Virginia's oldest plantation and is the oldest family-owned business in North

America, dating back to 1638.

A National Historic Landmark, the Shirley Plantation is known for its large collection of family portraits—dating back eleven generations. There's one particular portrait that's infamous among ghost hunters.

Seems that one of the family's aunts, known only as Aunt Pratt, still inhabits the manor and is quite picky about where her picture is hung. When the owners moved the portrait from its place downstairs, Aunt Pratt raised a real ruckus. Noises, particularly the sound of rocking in the attic, were heard late at night, until the owners could take no more. They moved the portrait back to its original spot. Seems Aunt Pratt is once again a happy—and quiet—ghost. The plantation is a major stop on Charles City's haunted plantations tour.

Shirley Plantation is Virginia's oldest plantation, settled in 1613.
Courtesy of Shirley Plantation/Williamsburg Area CVB

Located at 501 Shirley Plantation Road.

USS George Washington • Norfolk

This NIMITZ-class aircraft carrier is said to be haunted by a whole host of ghosts. The most peculiar apparition is that of a young girl, who has appeared often in the lower engineering levels of the ship. She seems to have quite a wardrobe stashed away down there, for sometimes she's wearing a pink and white dress and others, a blue one. She disappears when anyone tries to approach her.

There are reports of a ghostly man who disappears halfway down a flight of stairs and walks through equipment, and a ghost dog that disappears when approached. There are strange noises, such as the sound of keys jangling when no one is there, and strange happenings, such as phantom shoulder tapping, tools being moved, and the overwhelming sensation of being watched.

This is an active ship whose home port is Naval Station Norfolk.

Wayside Inn • Middletown

First opened in 1797, the Wayside Inn is one of the oldest inns in America. Just think of all the history that passed through its doors. During the

Wayside Inn is frequently visited by the ghosts of both Union and Confederate soldiers.
Photo by Keith Lanpher/ Courtesy of VTC

Civil War, Middletown was occupied at different times by both Confederate and Union soldiers, and the inn served as a hospital during these times. It is reported to be haunted by the ghosts of both Union and Confederate soldiers who died here. Room 14 seems to be especially active with strange noises and occurrences.

Located at 424 East Wisconsin Avenue.

Eat, Drink, and Be Merry!

Eating out in Strange But True Virginia is more than a meal—it's an experience. There are restaurants and bars galore along the back roads trail, some historic, some haunted, some just plain fun.

AUGUSTINE'S AT FREDERICKSBURG SQUARE • FREDERICKSBURG

Augustine's at Fredericksburg Square is known for its fine dining experience.
Photo by Weadon Photography, Fredericksburg, VA

From row house to mayoral mansion, to post office, to World War II induction center, to Elk's Lodge, this circa 1838 building has a long and storied history. Today, the building is home to fine dining. And, we do mean fine dining. The motto here ain't "No Shoes, No Shirt, No Service." It's "No Sandals, No Shorts, No Jeans. Please." If you simply must wear a T-shirt, it simply must be a designer T. So pull out your Sunday best and come on down.

The menu reads like a symphony. Consider a sample five-course meal: Start with Ragout of Petite Gris Escargots or, if money is no object, indulge yourself with Iranian Golden Osetra Caviar at $198 a pop. OK, well, it is served with Toasted Blini, Crème Fraîche, and two frozen Vodkas (to dull the pain to your budget?). After that, try the Oven Roasted Heirloom Beet Salad or maybe the Wilted Salad of Chicories. Next comes the entree, a nice Duet of Organic Lamb or the John Dory "En Pappillote," perhaps? Then, it's on to the cheese course, which includes an array of cheeses. And finally, it's the Finales (that's dessert to you and me). You can go for the really decadent, such as the Chocolate-Hazelnut Decadence Cake, or a bit lighter with the Warm Tart Tatin of Pineapple and Quince. Ummm…Ummm…Good.

White-gloved waiters serve you these fine meals in the restaurant's Victorian-era setting. Soft jazz music, low lights, and European linens and settings set the mood for a relaxing and romantic evening. It's fine dining at its best. So, save up!

Located at 525 Caroline Street.

Belmont Farm Distillery • Culpeper

Chuck and Jeanette Miller, the owners of Belmont Farm Distillery, come from a long line of Virginia distillers—better known as moonshiners. With their Virginia Lightning, they are preserving the family tradition.

The secret to making real Virginia Lightning, say the Millers, is in their genuine solid copper pot still, which preserves all the aroma and taste of fine corn whiskey. This method of whiskey making was abandoned throughout the country because of the time and care it takes.

Belmont Farm is the only distillery in the country to make its own brew from start to finish. The Millers grow, harvest, and grind their own corn. They then mix it with choice malt and cook it in a stainless steel cooker. Using an ol' family recipe, they cook the corn mash and send it for fermentation in that special 2000-gallon copper pot still, which was constructed in 1930. After distilling, the whiskey is bottled and sent to the state liquor stores for selling.

The distillery produces about 250 cases of corn whiskey per acre. They have two products: Copper Fox, a Virginia Whiskey; and the legal moonshine, Virginia Lightning Corn Whiskey.

Although Belmont has been making whiskey since 1989, it just opened to the public in October 2005. Tours of the farm and distillery are available. There's also a gift shop that sells the farm's products, T-shirts, and souvenirs. Don't go expecting a cheap high. Virginia state law prohibits sampling of the 100-proof libation!

Located at 13490 Cedar Run Road.

Chowning's Tavern • Williamsburg

Josiah Chowning opened his English alehouse tavern in 1776. His intent was to offer common folk "hearty food to replenish craving stomachs." That intent survives today, but current owners have added good fun to replenish craving souls.

Around 9:00 p.m., the tavern lights go up and the patrons are invited to engage in "gambols," eighteenth-century tavern games. The games are bawdy good fun, and you can join in if you wish, or sit by with a tankard of ale and enjoy the fun.

Food at Chowning's is hearty eighteenth-century fare—shepherd's pie, Brunswick stew, fish and chips, and cider cake. A wide variety of beers and snacks is also available.

Located at Duke of Gloucester Street.

Christiana Campbell's Tavern • Williamsburg

This is Williamsburg's most famous tavern, maybe because it's documented that George Washington ate here ten times. They even have a receipt! The April 8, 1772, document was written by Washington, using his quill pen to record his payment of seven pounds, seven shillings, and sixpence for his tab at Christiana Campbell. It's one of Colonial Williamsburg's most treasured documents.

During Washington's time, Campbell's was famous for its seafood, and it is again. The restaurant is an authentic restoration with eighteenth-century furnishings, a blazing fireplace, and flutists and balladeers to entertain diners.

Located on Waller Street.

Downtown Saloon aka Payne's Biker Café • Leesburg

The Downtown Saloon, which is also known as Payne's Biker Café, is a popular hangout for those free spirits who've discovered that life is more exciting when you're barreling through it astride 750 pounds of steel. The décor is early Harley-Davidson, with a laminated bar featuring pictures of local bikers in various stages of party mode, and stuff hanging from the ceiling. A neon sign on the outside window makes the droll observation Better Here Than Across The Street. A glance across said street at the local jail has you nodding in agreement.

The menu offers typical biker bar fare—pizza, meatball subs, and barbecue. And beer, the bikers' elixir.

For entertainment, there are pool tables and a DJ playing music from the 1950s to the 1990s, with live music on Saturday nights. So, if you're a little tired of all that dining amid history and don't mind partying with some rough-looking folks with hearts of gold, stop by Payne's. And, if you have a little too much of the biker's elixir, you can just wonder on across the street, and lock yourself in, Otis-style.

Located at Seven North King Street.

Did you know that Dr. Pepper was a real Virginia doctor? It seems that W.B. Morrison, manufacturer of the popular soft drink, worked as a pharmacist in a Rural Retreat drug store owned by Dr. Charles Pepper, an 1855 graduate of Virginia Medical School and a practicing physician in Rural Retreat.

Morrison moved to Waco, Texas, where he opened a drug store. Charles Alderton, a young pharmacist working at Morrison's store, developed a carbonated drink that was sold as a brain tonic and energizing drink. Morrison chose to name the drink after his former employer, possibly to give the drink more credibility. The Dr. Pepper Company was opened in 1885. It's the oldest soft drink manufacturing company in the country.

Gadsby's Tavern Museum • Alexandria

Named after Englishman John Gadsby, who operated a 1785 tavern and 1792 hotel here until 1808, the tavern and hotel were the center of Alexandria's economic, political, and social life in the late eighteenth and early nineteenth centuries.

The tavern was the setting for dancing, theatrical and musical performances, and meetings for local organizations. Its most notable celebration was Birthnight, the commemoration of George Washington's birthday. This event originated in England, when the monarch's birthday was celebrated with a party every year. Not wanting to miss out on the opportunity to party hardy, the colonists decided to continue the tradition after the American Revolution by celebrating Washington's birthday. And so, a new tradition was born! The birthday boy himself attended the Gadsby's ball in his honor in 1798.

Enjoy such hearty fare as Gentlemen's Pye, Spiced Filet of Cod, and George Washington's Favorite—a crispy half duckling with sage-cranberry stuffing—in one of the restaurant's three eighteenth-century dining rooms. A full selection of wines is available, and there is a Sunday brunch.

Don't be surprised if you have an uninvited guest while you're there. Diners often report seeing an apparition of a young woman dressed in 1800s clothing. Sightings have been so numerous that the proprietors conduct candlelight tours every Friday night.

Located at 134 North Royal Street.

Talk about not being able to make up your mind! In 1920, Iowan Christian Nelson didn't like deciding between candy or ice cream, so he invented the first chocolate-covered ice cream bar and named it the Eskimo Pie. Delicious, but what's it got to do with Virginia? Well, we're gonna tell ya.

In 1924, Nelson sold his Eskimo Pie Corporation to Reynolds' Metal in Richmond, which invented the bar's foil wrapper. Nelson worked as vice president and director of research of the Eskimo Pie division until 1961.

In 1992, the division became independent of Reynolds' Metal. The company is still headquartered in Richmond.

GRAYWOLF GRILL • RICHMOND

Looking for a wild dining experience? Try out the Graywolf Grill, a Mongolian restaurant. Wondering what wolves have to do with Mongolians? It's simple. Seems that back in the Ghengis Khan days, packs of wolves would follow the marauding hordes on their wild hunts, with both packs thrilling to the hunt. Afterward, the hordes would gather around the fire, cooking their meal and telling tall tales of the hunt.

You don't have to go to all that trouble for your meal at the Graywolf Grill. They've already hunted and dressed the meat for you. But you do get to create your own meal from the restaurant's array of five meats—chicken, beef, lamb, pork, and turkey. There's also shrimp, scallops, calamari, and shrimp.

Season it all with a selection of oils, sauces, and spices. And, afterward, you may feel like telling a tall tale or two.

Located at 1601 Willow Lawn Drive.

GREEN LEAFE CAFÉ • WILLIAMSBURG

According to *USA Today*, this is one of the ten best bars in the country. Williamsburg's only tap house, the Green Leafe offers thirty draft beers, one hundred bottled beers, a wide selection of Scotches, and more than forty wines from around the world. There's a cozy, friendly atmosphere, making the place a favorite with students (The College of William and Mary is across the street.) and locals.

Located at 765 Scotland Street.

HAUNTED DINNER THEATER • WILLIAMSBURG

Craving a little spooky adventure while you eat? Then the Haunted Dinner Theater is the place to be. Not only can you indulge in the seventy-one-item, all-you-can-eat buffet, but you can also enjoy a lot of spooky fun while you stuff your face.

Join in the interactive dinner show by helping to solve the haunted mystery. The lightning and thunder and other special effects give the joint a spooky atmosphere, and the performers dazzle you with their magic.

Located at 5363 Richmond Road.

INDIAN FIELDS TAVERN • CHARLES CITY

Nationally acclaimed in *Gourmet* and *Bon Appetit* magazines, Indian Fields Tavern is another of Virginia's finest fine dining restaurants. Located in the heart of Plantation Country, which includes five other Charles City County plantations, the turn-of-the-century farmhouse is surrounded by gardens in some of Virginia's most beautiful countryside.

The restaurant brags of using the freshest local ingredients, including, of course, Virginia hams, Chesapeake seafood, and herbs and vegetables grown on the premises. The menu reflects this local loyalty, with such items as Rappahannock Rockefeller, Grilled Local Quail, and Chesapeake Filet.

They also brag of Southern specialties, but we didn't see any fried chicken or country fried steak on the menu. Hmmm...Bet that quail would fry up quite nice. Add some black-eyed peas and mashed potatoes. ...

Located at 9220 John Tyler Memorial Highway.

IRELAND'S FOUR COURTS • ARLINGTON

Hankering for a wee bit o' the Irish? Well, drop on by Ireland's Four Courts, where their motto is Cead Mile Fialte (One Hundred Thousand Welcomes). This very popular establishment is the quintessential Irish pub, known for its low-key atmosphere, friendliness, and great beer.

Owner Jimmy Fagan, a County Cork native, has taken special pains in bringing a little of the Emerald Isle to Virginia. The décor is authentic, with a fireplace shipped from Dublin, Guinness posters, photos of Ireland plastered all around, and stout pewter mugs.

There's live music every night, with rousing Irish songs that will have you dancing a jig even before the Guinness starts nippin' at your feet. The food is hearty Irish fare, of course, with Shepherd's Pie, Chicken Innishmore, and Salmon of Knowledge, named for the Irish belief that salmon possesses the power of healing and the gift of wisdom.

Better come early, for this is a favorite with the locals, and it fills up fast—standing room only on Friday and Saturday nights.

Located at 2051 Wilson Boulevard.

LITTLE GRILL • HARRISONBURG

Oh! It's so ticky tacky! Operating as a restaurant since the 1940s, the Little Grill is filled with tacky treasures from years gone by, including a disembodied mannequin head, a broken tube-style radio, one crutch, and a treatise on relationships written by *Partridge Family* actress Susan Dey. What fun!

Little Grill operates as a soup kitchen one day a week.
Courtesy of Little Grill

Food at the Little Grill is healthy fare. Although they do offer real meat burgers and chicken, turkey, and ham sandwiches, most offerings are sans meat. You'll find such palatable dishes as bean burritos wrapped in freshly made tortillas, fried potatoes blanketed in corn tortillas, stir-fried vegetables, and falafel.

The price is right, too. Hardly anything exceeds $7. It's even better on Mondays, when the owners convert the restaurant into a soup kitchen. Everything is free. It's more a community offering, say the owners, than a charity meal. Everyone is welcome to come and eat, and if you'd like, you can help cook, serve, and clean. More fun!

Located at 621 North Main Street.

ABC Bakers is the oldest licensed baker of Girl Scout cookies in the country. The Richmond company has been baking those delicious little goodies since 1939, when shortbread and those cute circle cookies with the hole in the middle were the only varieties offered.

Today, there is a variety of Girl Scout cookies, and ABC Bakers provides almost half of the country's supply of them, which are among the country's top fifteen sellers. If you've got a craving, take a tour of the bakery for a few samples.

Mystery Dinner Playhouse • Richmond/ Virginia Beach/ Williamsburg

It's a mystery. Won't be for long, though, when you sup at the Mystery Dinner Playhouse. All during your meal, you'll have the opportunity to play super sleuth and figure out just who among you done it.

As you enter the joint, you're greeted by one of the surly suspects, who seats you and prepares you for the soon-to-unfold mystery. With action taking place throughout the room, a four-course dinner is served by a zany cast of characters—suspects all.

Keep those peepers peeled for clues and jot them down, so's youse don't forget them. As the plot thickens, you'll receive a clue dossier containing, among other things, bribe money to grease those suspects' palms for better clues. You also get the opportunity to give 'em the ol' third degree as they serve you between scenes.

At Mystery Dinner Playhouse, guests can help solve a murder.
Photo by Laura Daab

At the end of the evening, you're given the opportunity to solve the mystery, and a prize is awarded for the Super Sleuth who puts it all together. If you're clueless, hey, just take a guess. There's also a prize for the most creative answer. And if you just can't come up with anything original, you can always just tell 'em the butler done it.

You can solve the mystery at any of three locations: 9826 Midlothian Turnpike, Richmond; 1900 Pavilion Drive, Virginia Beach; or 5351 Richmond Road, Williamsburg.

NAPOLEON'S RESTAURANT • WARRENTON

Another mystery is why this restaurant is named for that French emperor. For all the rich history surrounding Warrenton, we're purt near certain that ol' Nappy never made a visit here.

Regardless, the restaurant named in his honor has offered fine dining since 1978 and has added casual dining in the Napoleon's Café section. Built in the 1830s, the Greek Revival building holds a prominent place in Warrenton's history. During the Civil War, it was owned by Judge William H. Gaines, a later presiding justice of the Fauquier County Court. Still later, it was owned by General Eppa Hunton, who served in the U.S. House of Representatives and the U.S Senate after the Civil War.

Located at 67 Waterloo (where else?) Street.

PAINTED LADY • NORFOLK

This bright restaurant is aptly named. Washed in vivid pinks, lavenders, and greens, it does remind one of a slightly gaudy woman. Despite that, the atmosphere is genteel, with period furnishings, a full service bar constructed of rare exotic woods, and five original fireplaces, which are credited with garnering the Lady the Most Romantic Restaurant award.

The Painted Lady has been named the Most Romantic Restaurant. Courtesy of the Painted Lady

In addition to lunch, dinner, and Sunday brunch, the Lady offers several versions of that age-old tradition, afternoon tea. There's the Cream Tea, with scones and Devonshire cream; British Afternoon Tea, with finger sandwiches, scones, and raspberry chocolates; and the Royal Tea, a full-course tea that includes champagne, sherry, or port. A favorite is the Teddy Bear Tea especially for children, with peanut butter and jelly sandwiches and assorted fruits.

Located at 112 East 17th Street.

Poe's Pub • Richmond

Named for poet Edgar Allan Poe, this quirky Irish pub is considered one of Richmond's best places for live music. On any given night, you can find anything from small bands to acoustic performers, to loud and flashy bands. The music style runs the gamut: blues, rock, country, alternative, bluegrass, zydeco, with a little surfer music thrown in for good measure. It's loud. It's smoky. It's full of attitude.

The food is as sassy as the music: baby back ribs, catfish sub, tuna steak sandwich, salmon filet, blue cheese burgers, and gourmet grilled cheese. It's an all around entertaining evening, one you'll never consider dark and dreary.

Located at 2706 East Main Street.

Rainforest Café • McLean

And you thought it was endangered! Not so. The Rainforest is alive and well and is thriving in McLean. Bring along the kiddies, for they're the ones who'll enjoy this dining adventure most.

Entering the Rainforest Café is like stepping into a kitschy version of a tropical jungle, complete with the shadowy darkness and all the sights and sounds. Real parrots shriek at you from the huge fake trees and plants that cover every inch of the restaurant. There's thunder crashing, lightning flashing, and rain pouring down in strategic places. As you safari your way to your table, gorillas, crocodiles, snakes, and other jungle animals peer at you from flora, all going nuts at synchronized intervals.

Safari guides serve you from the extensive menu that includes appetizers, salads, pizza, burgers, sandwiches, meatloaf, steak, stir-fry, and pasta. Present an ID and you can get a doctored-up drink from the ol' medicine man at the bar. And you're probably going to need it, because after all that jungle overload, the kids aren't going to let you bypass the animal-themed gift shop, conveniently located on the way out.

Located at 7928 L. Tyson's Corner Center.

Rosie Rumpe's Regal Dumpe Dinner Theatre • Williamsburg

Leave the kids at home (you did take them to the Rainforest Café, after all), and join Henry VIII for some bawdy fun at his favorite tavern. Located within the Maple Tree Restaurant, Rosie Rumpe's is the most boisterous three hours you'll find anywhere.

From your first step inside, you'll find yourself amid lusty serving wenches, wandering minstrels, and foolish court jesters. Join in the lively fun, dance, bang on the tables, but don't get too rowdy, or you'll end up in the stocks.

If you're really lucky, perhaps ol' King Henry will stop in. A jovial man, he has a fondness for food and drink—and even more fondness for pretty women. So, have fun all you comely wenches, just be careful you don't lose your heads!

Located at 1665 Richmond Road.

That dapper peanut icon, Mr. Peanut, is a native Virginian. He was the brainchild of thirteen-year-old Suffolk, Virginia, resident Antonio Gentile, who entered a logo contest sponsored by Planter's Peanuts in 1916. The logo was intended to advertise the world's first commercially-sold roasted peanuts.

Antonio's original drawing, which won him the huge sum of $5, depicted a peanut man with crossed arms and legs, who Antonio dubbed "Mr. Peanut." A professional illustrator later added the top hat, monocle, white gloves, and cane to give the icon a more upscale look.

Drive by the Planter's plant in Suffolk and get a gander at the life-size statue and fourteen cast-iron statues that line the fence around the processing facility. You can also purchase Mr. Peanut collectibles, such as salt and pepper shakers.

Strawberry Street Café • Richmond

This Richmond café has a unique draw. In its center, sits the salad bar. But, it's not just any salad bar. It's a bathtub. Yep, the fresh vegetables, fruits, and prepared salads all sit temptingly on a bed of ice in a big, old-fashioned claw foot bathtub. Guess they must be really clean. The salad tub recently brought national attention to the restaurant, when an answer in the popular game show *Jeopardy!* read: The Strawberry Street Café in this Virginia capital is famous for its bathtub salad bar. The question of course was, "What is Richmond?"

The décor of the café matches the claw foot tub, with intricate stained glass, rich woodwork, and antique mirrors. Open for lunch and dinner, the café menu includes burgers, quiche, pasta, seafood, chicken, steak, and a wide variety of desserts.

Located at 421 North Strawberry Street.

The Tobacco Company Restaurant • Richmond

The Shockoe Slip district of Richmond was once the vital headquarters of the city's tobacco and cotton barons, who traded in the port below the falls of James River. The district was almost destroyed during the Civil War, and though it was briefly revived, it gradually deteriorated.

In 1973, farseeing businessman Jearald Cable had a vision of the area as a major retail and restaurant district, a vision he began by securing several old warehouses and designing a restaurant that embodied the Victorian era of the original Shockoe Slip district, when tobacco was king.

The restoration of that warehouse became the Tobacco Company Restaurant, whose focal point is a three-story atrium with an exposed antique Otis elevator that carries customers from the first floor cocktail lounge to the two upstairs dining rooms.

The furnishings throughout are authentic Victorian-era, including the stairway that was salvaged from Richmond's ol' St. Luke's Hospital, a large wooden Indian carved by a South Carolina craftsman, and a brass chandelier from the Federal Reserve Bank in Cincinnati. Add hundreds of plants and fresh flowers, and you have a historically rich and beautiful landmark.

The restaurant offers fine dining for lunch, dinner, and Sunday brunch. Reservations are required for dinner. Live music is featured in the first floor bar Tuesday through Saturday nights.

Located within the restaurant, but with a separate entrance, is an exclusive nightclub that's open Thursday, Friday, and Saturday nights only. Its interior is the same stained glass, rich wood, antique-filled décor as the restaurant. There's also a state-of-the-art sound system and a large dance floor.

The restaurant is located at 1201 East Cary Street.

Virginia Diner • Wakefield

This seventy-five-year-old diner began life in a refurbished Sussex, Surry, and Southampton Railroad car. Business grew after a dining room was added. It was during those days that the diner began a tradition that survives today. Customers are greeted by antique peanut roasters with buckets of free peanuts to munch while they wait. The peanuts come fresh from the fields of Wakefield, Virginia's Peanut Capital.

Today, the railroad diner, though faithfully replicated, is a fond memory, but not the good Southern home cooking that made the Virginia Diner so popular. Fried chicken and pork chops, country-fried steak, black-eyed peas, green beans, candied yams, and biscuits are all menu staples. You'll also find favorite dessert items, such as peach cobbler and apple pie, though you may want to go for the peanut pie, a local favorite.

Virginia Diner has been serving up Southern cuisine for seventy-five years.
Photo by Bill Galloway, Virginia Diner

Located on Route 460.

Jamestown, the first of the original thirteen colonies, was founded for the purpose of cultivating silk to be traded with the court of King James. After a fungus destroyed the mulberry trees, which fed the silkworms, tobacco was planted as a cash crop.

Bigfoot: A Big Thing in Virginia

There's a hairy creature inhabiting the back woods of Virginia, and no, it's not Uncle Buddy off on a toot. Might be Aunt Thelma, though. This creature is reportedly sheep-dog-hairy, eight-feet tall, and weighs in at around four hundred pounds. Smells bad, too. Yep, sounds a lot like Auntie T.

According to the Virginia Bigfoot Research Organization, Virginia lays claim to some of the oldest Bigfoot sightings on record, dating back to the 1880s. They should know. The organization was founded to combine "scientific methodology and shamanistic awareness in hopes of establishing peaceful contact with the wonderful creatures." Their website at www.virginiabigfootresearch.org contains a wealth of Virginia Bigfoot sightings.

Miscellaneous Miscellany

It's The Law!

Better watch your step in our Strange But True Virginia. You never know when the long arm of the law may reach out and nab you for breaking some of these strange but true laws!

1. It's illegal to hunt on Sundays, except for raccoons, which can be hunted until 2:00 a.m. But, officer, I swear. Those antlers looked just like ears in that spotlight!
2. Sexual relations are illegal if you're not married. Hey, baby, let's go to Vegas. Kiss the single life goodbye!
3. It's illegal to have sex with the lights on. Light the candles, darlin'.
4. It's also illegal to have sex in any other position than missionary. Oops!
5. It's illegal to tickle women. Stop that now, before I have to call 911!
6. In Culpeper, it's illegal to wash your mule on the sidewalk. But look at him, officer. He's filthy!
7. It's illegal to kick your wife out of bed in Lebanon. Wake up, honey. The cops are here.

8. Spitting on a seagull is illegal in Norfolk. It's just not fair, officer! Look what he dropped on me!
9. In Prince William County, it's illegal to have a skunk as a pet. Oh, but, officer, he's just so cute. Ewww!
10. In Norfolk, women must wear a corset after sundown and be in the company of a male chaperon. Fat chance.
11. There's a state law prohibiting "corrupt practices of bribery by any person other than candidates." Obviously, it's OK for the candidate.
12. A Virginia law requires all bathtubs to be kept out in yards, and not inside houses.

Towns of Note

Virginia has its share of towns with strange names—Butts, Fagg, and Frogtown, to name just a few—and it's also got towns notable for some unique things.

Eight presidents of the United States claim Virginia as their places of birth: George Washington, Thomas Jefferson, James Madison, James Monroe, William Henry Harrison, John Tyler, Zachary Taylor, and Woodrow Wilson. Six presidents' wives were born here: Martha Washington, Martha Jefferson, Rachel Jackson, Letitia Tyler, Ellen Arthur, and Edith Wilson.

Appomattox

The Civil War ended here on April 8, 1865. General Robert E. Lee surrendered to General Ulysses S. Grant on the steps of the town's courthouse, which is now part of a National Historic Park.

The Appomattox Court House was the site of surrender for General Robert E. Lee.
Photo by Keith Lanpher/Courtesy of VTC

Big Stone Gap

This quirky town is the setting for a series of best-selling books by author Adriana Trigiani, who grew up in Big Stone Gap in the 1970s. The books are about fictional pharmacist Ava Maria Mulligan, who worked at the Mutual Pharmacy and served as a director for the Trail of the Lonesome Pine outdoor theater. Visit Big Stone Gap and see other landmarks featured in the books and talk to the townsfolk, who love discussing them and their bizarre characters.

Bristol

Bristol has a split personality. Half of the town lies in Virginia and half lies in Tennessee. Each half has its own government and city services.

Chincoteague

Among other things, Chincoteague is the Clam Capital of the World.

Forest

This is the home of Poplar Forest, the inherited plantation of Thomas Jefferson's wife, Martha. The working tobacco farm of more than four thousand acres provided Jefferson with a significant portion of his income.

Thomas Jefferson enjoyed reading, writing, and gardening at Poplar Forest.
Courtesy of Thomas Jefferson's Poplar Forest

Jefferson, who studied architecture, considered his home an architectural triumph. The octagonal design was unique for the time and was something Jefferson found much satisfaction in. After retiring from public office, Jefferson often came to Poplar Forest to get away from the bustle of Monticello, and enjoy a few secluded pastimes, such as reading, writing, and gardening.

After years of neglect, the home has been restored to its former glory and is open for tours.

Located at 158 Bateman Bridge Road.

Gloucester

In May 2003, archeologists announced the discovery of the lost Indian Village Werowocomoco on a farm near Gloucester. This was the principal village of the powerful chief Powhatan. It was here that Pocahontas saved Captain John Smith's bacon by throwing her body over his to keep her father, Chief Powhatan, from executing him.

Gordonsville

Gordonsville claims to be the Fried Chicken Capital of the World.

Hillsville

In 1912, the courthouse of this small town was the site of a good ol' Western-style shoot-out. Seems that local citizen Floyd Allen had just been sentenced to one year in jail for assault on a police officer. As the officers proceeded to escort him to jail, Floyd stood up and declared he wasn't going. Reaching into his pocket for what turned out to be some papers, he was shot at by the clerk of the court. Floyd's brother, Sidna, and his son, Claude, pulled guns and fired. The prosecuting attorney and deputy clerk pulled their guns and fired, bringing a return volley from two of Floyd's nephews, Wesley Edwards and Friel Allen, and ending with shots from five deputy sheriffs.

The shoot-out lasted two minutes, and resulted in five deaths and the wounding of seven others. The judge, the sheriff, the prosecuting attorney, a juryman, and a witness were all killed in the crossfire. Floyd and Claude were sentenced to death by electrocution, Sidna received thirty-five years in prison, Wesley twenty-seven years, and Friel eighteen years.

The courthouse, still bullet ridden, is in use today.

LEXINGTON

Lexington is home to two excellent educational institutions. Virginia Military Institute was founded in 1839, and is the country's oldest state-supported military college. During the Civil War, on May 15, 1864, the VMI Corps of Cadets served as a unit in a battle at New Market, Virginia. They were credited with turning the tide in favor of the Confederates there. In retaliation, most of the institute was shelled and burned by Union forces on June 12, 1864. General Stonewall Jackson was a professor at VMI for ten years before the Civil War, and General George C. Marshall, World War II Army Chief of Staff, was a 1901 graduate.

Washington and Lee University was founded as Augusta Academy in 1749.
Courtesy of the Lexington & Rockbridge Area Tourism Development

Washington and Lee University is the nation's ninth oldest institute of higher learning. It was founded in 1749 as Augusta Academy, and was renamed Liberty Hall in 1776. President

George Washington rescued the struggling college in 1796, when he donated the first endowment of $20,000 in James River Canal Stock. It was renamed in his honor in 1813. The college was again renamed (for the last time?) in 1871 to include Robert E. Lee, who served as president of the university from 1865 until his death in 1870.

The two colleges meld into one another at the center of Lexington.

LYNCHBURG

Lynchburg was the part-time home of Dr. Malcolm Loomis, who, in October 1868, used a vertical antenna, a high frequency detector, and a spark gap transmitter to successfully send electromagnetic waves through the atmosphere. In case you aren't electronics savvy (we aren't), this means that Dr. Loomis invented the radio six years before the reputed Father of Radio Guglielmo Marconi was even born. Unfortunately, Loomis lacked the funds to perfect his equipment and gain recognition for his invention.

Lynchburg was the part-time home of Dr. Malcolm Loomis.
Courtesy of the City of Lynchburg—Communications and Marketing

Middleburg

Middleburg is a horsey town. It is, in fact, the nation's horse and hunt capital. Many of the nation's top equestrians, including Olympic medal contenders, are stabled here. You can enjoy all things equine here, from steeplechases to polo matches, to stable tours, to riding lessons.

Middleburg is the nation's horse and hunt capital.
Photo by Jeff Greenberg/Courtesy of VTC

If horses aren't your thing, don't despair. There's some celebrity watching to be done. Actor Robert Duvall and weatherman Willard Scott are residents who might be glimpsed at the local Safeway, one of the few Safeways in the nation with chandeliers.

Spotsylvania

General Stonewall Jackson was accidentally shot in the arm here in 1863. It was amputated two inches below the shoulder in a field hospital. Jackson died one week later from complications, and his body, minus the arm, was buried at Virginia Military Institute.

For some reason, his arm was buried separately. It was given an honorable burial at the Ellwood Plantation, fifteen miles west of Fredericksburg. A marker on the site reads simply, "Arm of Stonewall Jackson. May 3."

STAUNTON

Staunton is the birthplace of U.S. President Woodrow Wilson, and is the location of the Woodrow Wilson Presidential Library. Included in the site is Woodrow Wilson's birthplace home, the Woodrow Wilson Museum, and the Woodrow Wilson Gardens.

Located at 18-24 North Coalter Street.

YORKTOWN

In September of 1781, most of the forces of the American Revolution converged on Yorktown. The British Royal Navy was defeated on September 5, 1781, in the Battle of Chesapeake Bay, an action that cut off British General Cornwallis's supplies and transportation.

Hearing of the defeat, Washington quickly moved his troops from New York to Yorktown, and with combined forces of seventeen thousand troops, began the Battle of Yorktown on October 6. By October 19, it was all over but the crying for the British. And Cornwallis must've been doing some crying. Seems he was too embarrassed by his defeat to do the manly thing and surrender in person. Instead, claiming to be ill, he sent a subordinate to do the surrendering for him. Military protocol, in turn, dictated that Washington also send a subordinate. He sent General Benjamin Lincoln to accept the surrender.

Today, the Yorktown battlefield is maintained as Colonial National Park, which includes historic Jamestown and the Colonial Parkway, which connects the historic triangle of Jamestown, Williamsburg, and Yorktown.

A National Park Service Ranger in Yorktown tells a group of visitors about the home of Thomas Nelson Jr.
Courtesy of Colonial National Historical Park/Williamsburg Area CVB

Funny Happenings Here

Pigs in the park. Pirates in the bay. Puppies on parade. There's just no end to the funny goings on in Strange But True Virginia.

American Indian Festival Powwow • Chesapeake

Wow. A powwow in the park. Ever wondered just what a powwow was? Well, we're gonna tell ya anyway. The term "powwow" is an English mangling of the Algonquian word "pauwau," a word that was once used to describe medicine men and spiritual leaders.

Periodically during each year, tribes of Native Americans would hold a spiritual gathering—perhaps something like a Baptist revival—to celebrate their heritage and spirituality. It's a time to sing and dance, and a time to renew old friendships and create new ones. Because these festival-like events had strong religious overtones, the medicine men and spiritual leaders played a big role in them.

The early settlers, however, thought the word "pauwau" described the entire event. When Native Americans learned English, they probably thought it was too difficult to explain to these dumb palefaces the exact meaning (and spelling) of the word, and so they accepted the new meaning of powwow.

Today, powwows are held all over the country, none more interesting or fun than Chesapeake's American Indian Festival, held annually in June. The celebration features American Indian storytelling, traditional dances, and demonstrations in native dress. There are also Native American jewelry and crafts, and Native American and traditional food.

Held in the Chesapeake City Park at 500 Greenbrier Parkway.

APPALACHIAN FOLK FESTIVAL • ROANOKE

Nestled between the Appalachian and Blue Ridge Mountains, the Shenandoah Valley is the heart of Virginia's mountain culture. At the Appalachian Folk Festival, you can immerse yourself in a wholly different way of life, enriched by a unique musical and cultural heritage. The festival takes you through three centuries—1600s, 1700s, and 1800s—of Appalachian culture, including traditional music, historical demonstrations, games, storytelling, and crafts.

Traditional entertainer Ken Bloom sits with his concert zither on the porch of the 1850 Hofauger House at the Appalachian Folk Festival. Courtesy of Explore Park

Held in April in Explore Park at Milepost 115, Blue Ridge Parkway.

Apple Dumpling Festival • Stuart

With 18,600 acres of apple farms, Virginia ranks sixth in the nation for apple production. In 2000, 350 million pounds of apples were produced, including the state's five leading varieties—Red Delicious, York, Golden Delicious, Rome, and Fuji.

It's no wonder, then, that there are apple festivals across the state. Stuart's Apple Dumpling Festival is held in the town's historic Depot district, where there are live bands, arts and crafts, and plenty of good food. The star of the festival, of course, is the apple dumpling, a sweet, cinnamony pastry concoction stuffed with juicy baked apples.

Held in October at The Depot on South Main Street.

Blue Ridge Folklife Festival • Ferrum

One of the country's largest celebrations of regional traditions, the Blue Ridge Folklife Festival was named to the Top 20 Events in the Southeast by the Southeast Tourism Society in 1997. Every year, more than fifteen thousand people revel in the sights and sounds of old-time Blue Ridge during the one-day extravaganza, which is held in October on the Ferrum College campus.

One event at the Blue Ridge Folklife Festival is the Coon Mule Jumping Contest.
Photo by Ken McCreedy/Courtesy of Blue Ridge Institute & Museum of Ferrum College

Three stages showcase traditional music. There's a stage for sacred music, one for string bands, and a Blue Ridge Heritage stage that features country blues, rockabilly, and old-time traditional.

Above the music, you'll hear the mournful baying of working dogs used for hunting, and the comical braying of the mules that once were used for plowing fields. There are also folk crafts, storytelling, food, and cars.

Held at the Blue Ridge Institute and Museum of Ferrum College on Route 40.

Brunswick Stew Festival • Richmond

Wanna get stewed? Then come to the Brunswick Stew Festival, held every year in November. Not only will you enjoy some of the best Brunswick stew you've ever tasted, but you'll also get to party hardy.

Brunswick stew, which Brunswick County, Virginia, claims to have invented (a claim disputed by Brunswick, Virginia), was originally made with squirrel, but chicken is now the meat of choice. Throw in corn, tomatoes, and either okra, peas, or lima beans, and you have a hearty Southern stew.

The Brunswick Stew Festival awards prizes in two categories: Best Traditional Recipe and Most Original Recipe, in which anything goes. One year there was even a Big Bird Stew, a recipe featuring emu.

In addition to all the cooking and eating, there are live music, jugglers, musicians, and a petting zoo.

Held in the 17th Street Farmers' Market.

Cabbage Festival at Poor Farmers Farm • Vesta

Home fried cabbage, pinto beans, and corn bread. Fried pies for dessert. Ummm...ummm....ummm... There's just nothing better on the planet. And, it's what you'll find at the Cabbage Festival at Poor Farmers Farm.

There's also bluegrass music to listen to and enjoy—dance if the spirit moves you. And when you're all danced out, take home some of that good ol' Southern food to enjoy later. Just don't forget the Beano!

Located at 7958 JEB Stuart Highway.

Carter Family Traditional Music Festival • Hiltons

Native Virginians, the Carter family is the most influential group in country music history. Originally comprised of gaunt, shy Alvin P. Carter; his wife, Sara; and their sister-in-law, "Mother" Maybelle, the group sang a simple harmony that switched the emphasis of bluegrass from hillbilly instrumentals to vocals, and influenced other bluegrass family groups of the 1930s and 1940s. They also influenced folk and rock musicians, such as Woody Guthrie, the Kingston Trio, Bob Dylan, and Emmylou Harris. Through several generations, the Carter family tradition has endured and expanded to include daughters and granddaughters.

The Carter Family Traditional Music Festival, held the first weekend in August, honors the original Carter family group and celebrates the family's musical tradition. While you're there, visit the Carter Family Museum in the old general store building and the recently restored cabin that was the birthplace of Alvin Carter.

Located on Route 614.

COURT DAYS FESTIVAL • HARRISONBURG

Back in the olden days, say the 1850s, Court Days—days when court was held—were big events in Harrisonburg. They were days of commerce and socializing, when trials and sentencing were good excuses to get together.

The Court Days Festival relives those good ol' days, with reenactments of trials, an evening ball, old-fashioned games, and much more. There are even ballroom dancing lessons, so you won't embarrass yourself in the Grand Ballroom.

Held annually in June. Located at One Court Square.

EASTERN SHORE BIRDING AND WILDLIFE FESTIVAL • CAPE CHARLES

If vegetables, music, or litigation don't do it for you, how 'bout chirpy little birdies? Come to Virginia's Eastern Shore in October for the annual gathering of songbirds and raptors. The birds amass in huge numbers, resting a bit before their long flight to the tropics, providing an incredible opportunity for bird lovers.

The Birding and Wildlife Festival is held during this fall migration, not only celebrating the birds and wildlife of the area, but also educating visitors on the birds and the importance of protecting their habitat. OK, so they don't have music, but they do have live entertainment. There are millions of birds, singing and flitting and darting. There are birding and butterfly tours, safari boating trips, marsh and woodland hikes, a hawk observatory, bat and owl studies, sea grasses and oyster reef trips. It's nature lovers' heaven.

Held in Kiptopeke State Park at 3540 Kiptopeke Drive.

Five-Alarm Festival • Hampton

"Fire! Water! Water!" That'll be the cry as you sample the entries in this chili cook-off. The festival celebrates firefighters and the hard work they do putting their lives on the line for others. Held in conjunction with Fire Prevention week, it kicks off with a fire parade, featuring fire trucks and equipment.

After the parade, you can head on down to Mill Park to help judge the chili cook-off. There are three divisions: Restaurants, Fire Stations, and Open Competition. Awards are given for the best chili in each division. You can help decide the People's Choice Award by donating to the chili pot of your favorite sample. One hundred percent of these donations go to the Children's Hospital of the King's Daughters Pediatric Trauma Center to treat burn victims. The People's Choice winner receives the Soon-To-Be-Coveted Gold Chili Pot. It's a sizzling good time.

Held in Downtown Hampton's Mill Point Park at 100 Eaton Street.

Fredericksburg Dog Festival • Fredericksburg

Once a year, the city of Fredericksburg goes to the dogs. During the Dog Festival, more than two hundred dogs and their humans parade through downtown Fredericksburg and participate in various competitions for a full day of doggy fun. Prizes are awarded for such attributes as the fluffiest tail, the best spots, the blackest nose, and the largest puppy. There are obedience and trick contests, and costume contests, with participants transforming themselves into pirates, princesses, aliens, and handymen.

The highlight of the event is the crowning of the Sweetheart Queen, which is open to doggies of both genders. The only requirement is that your pooch be wearing appropriate queen attire.

Held in October in Hurkamp Park.

Dressed as the Queen of Hearts, this canine hopes to win a costume contest at the Fredericksburg Dog Festival.
Photo by Sonja Wise/Fredericksburg Parks and Recreation Department

Hampton Blackbeard Festival • Hampton

Yo, Ho, Ho! And a bottle of rum! The Blackbeard Festival takes you back to 1718, back to the time when Hampton was a bustling port city. The town's customs house regulated the export of tobacco to England and all of the manufactured commodities imported to the colonies. This wealth of loot floating around in the bay made Hampton a target for some of the most fearsome pirates of the Caribbean, including one—the most feared of all—who had declared himself a changed man.

Edward Drummond, aka Edward Teach, aka Blackbeard the Pirate, had grown tired of the roving life of a buccaneer. Moving to North Carolina with his fourteenth wife, he persuaded the governor to give him a pardon and began to live the life of a gentleman. Ah, but the call of the sea is a powerful thing—or at least the call of untold wealth.

Under the aegis of North Carolina's governor, Drummond began to venture out periodically, relieving ships of their cargoes—salvaging abandoned cargoes, he claimed—which he split with the governor. By 1718, he dropped all pretenses and resumed his life of violence, targeting ships and citizens along Chesapeake Bay. During this year, he hosted the most notorious pirate festival ever on the beach at Ocracoke Inlet. Here, he was joined by the most infamous pirates and their crews, including Hampton's own William Howard, one of Blackbeard's captains. They feasted and drank rum spiked with gun powder (sounds like that could have an explosive ending!).

Governor Spotswood of Virginia, tired of all the looting and convinced that the governor of North Carolina was protecting the pirates, planned an expedition to capture or kill Blackbeard. He named Lt. Robert Maynard to head the expedition and gave him two small ships to complete the mission.

Maynard and his crew found Blackbeard and engaged in a bloody battle to the death, during which Blackbeard received twenty-five mortal wounds (hmmm…sounds like overkill), and was slain when Maynard finally severed his head. The head was placed on a stake at the entrance to the Hampton River, at what's now known as Blackbeard's Point. Legend has it that Blackbeard still wanders around the point looking for his lost head.

Blackbeard does, indeed, sail the waters of the Hampton River the first weekend in June, for that's the weekend of the Blackbeard Festival, the highlight of which is a reenactment of the story we just told you. There are tall sailing ships, pirates, wenches, and soldiers. And you can join in if you want.

History buffs can join John Glass and his authentic "living history pirate crew." To be a part of this crew and join the reenactment, your dress has to be authentic "from the buckles on your shoes to the top of your tricorn hat." For a little more lax participation, you can join the "polyester pirates," where the dress is just whatever you think a pirate outfit should be. You can then work and play as a pirate in any area of the festival except the living history section.

HANOVER TOMATO FESTIVAL • MECHANICSVILLE

You say tomato and we say maters. Whatever you call them, there's nothing better than a good ol' mater samich with bacon and lettuce.

The Hanover Tomato Festival is a celebration of the juicy little fruit (yes, the tomato is a fruit, not a vegetable) grown in Hanover County. It's earned a reputation throughout Virginia for its unique flavor and texture. It's Hanover's sandy soil, growers believe, that give the Hanover tomato its succulence. At least

Looking to win the title Best Dressed, a small tomato eagerly awaits a decision during the tomato-decorating contest of the Hanover Tomato Festival.
Photo by Devin Brown

that's their story, and they're sticking to it. They're not giving away any growing secrets.

The festival features a tomato cooking contest, arts and crafts, live music, and children's activities.

Held in July at Pole Green Park at 8996 Pole Green Park Lane.

Hot Glass Festival • Staunton

OK. Here's a festival you don't see every day. Learn how glass products are made, and watch Virginia's finest hot glass artists demonstrate the various hot glass techniques, including traditional glassblowing, sand casting, and lamp working. Virginia's finest hot glass artists will be exhibiting their work. It's a rare opportunity to buy work from so many hot glass artists in one place.

Held in April at Sunspots Studios at 202 South Lewis Street.

Juneteenth Emancipation Celebration • Newport News

President Abraham Lincoln's Emancipation Proclamation freed the slaves on January 1, 1863, but word of the proclamation didn't reach Texas until June 1865. Legend has it that the bearer of the news rode a very slow mule all the way, and that's why it took two years for the news to reach Texas. Uh-huh. Historians know that many slave owners knew of the proclamation but refused to tell their slaves.

There's no stopping progress, however, and so finally, on June 19, 1865, Major General Gordon Granger stood on the balcony of Aston Villa in Galveston and read the proclamation declaring slaves to be free and equal to their owners.

June 19—Juneteenth for short—immediately became a day of celebration for African Americans in Texas until the Civil Rights Movement in the 1960s. It once again became popular in the 1970s.

The Juneteenth Emancipation Celebration commemorates the date slaves were freed in Texas.
Courtesy of The Newsome House Museum & Cultural Center, Newport News, VA

The Juneteenth Freedom Festival is a celebration of the event. You'll learn the history of Juneteenth through reenactments with live interpreters, who tell the story of how the slaves of Galveston, Texas, did not learn of their freedom until two years after the Emancipation Proclamation was adopted. There are evening events, music, food, and fun.

Held in June (when else?), the celebration begins at The Newsome House Museum and Cultural Center (2803 Oak Avenue), and later continues at the James A. Field House at 617 27th Street.

MANASSAS CHOCOLATE FESTIVAL • MANASSAS

At the Manassas Chocolate Festival, you can indulge your passion for chocolate. Start out with a pancake breakfast and later enter your own special recipe in the chocolate bake-off. There are chocolate fountains, a chocolate buffet, samplings of chocolate from around the world, and hands-on children's activities. End the day with an evening of champagne and chocolate. You'll be stuffed, loving, and drunk! What a day!

Held in November at 8957 Center Street.

NEPTUNE FESTIVAL BOARDWALK WEEKEND • VIRGINIA BEACH

Let's partaay! The Neptune Festival is the last and biggest blast of the season, a boisterous, rowdy send-off to summer. For three days and three nights, there's a whole host of party activities. Like playing in the sand? Then come to the internationally-known North American Sandsculpting Competition and watch as master sculptors mold sand into masterpieces. Dance and sing along the thirty blocks of tented stages featuring live music. Enjoy the art of more than 250 artisans. Eat, drink, and be merry with a veritable smorgasbord of food and drink.

There's also a parade and all sorts of athletic competitions, including an 8K run, a volleyball competition, a surfing competition, and a recreational sailing day. Events for the kids include a Youth Day, with jugglers, musicians, shoreline games, and a Youth Art Show. And don't miss the fireworks!

Held the last weekend in September on Virginia Beach Oceanfront between 2nd and 31st Street.

Pigs in the Park • Danville

Barbecue is Southern, right down to its little piggy toes. Ain't nothin' better than a big ol' slab of ribs cooked slow over an open pit and brushed lovingly with Aunt Maybelle's secret sauce. But the search is always on to find a recipe that comes close.

That's the idea behind Pigs in the Park. We'll come clean here—there really are no pigs in the park. At least not live ones. The pigs are actually all sizzling on the grill in this annual barbecue cook-off. More than forty contestants from five states come here to compete for prizes of more than $15,000 and prove their recipes to be the most delectable. You can enjoy the competition and sample some of the world's best barbecue.

Held in May in Ballou Park.

Pork, Peanut, and Pine Festival • Surry

The three Ps? Yep, three of Virginia's top products are celebrated in this two-day festival. Held at the Chippokes Plantation State Park, this festival features more than 225 artisans displaying their wares throughout the plantation's gardens. You'll find baskets, needlework, handcrafted furniture, quilts, wood carvings, dolls, birdhouses, wind chimes, and ornaments.

Enjoy pig in all its edible forms, from barbecue to chops to cracklings to chitterlings (oh, yuck!). To go along with it, there is plenty of traditional food fare, including kettle corn, funnel cakes, and apple pie.

Other activities include working demonstrations and

exhibits on pork products, peanuts, and pines. There's a working sawmill, chain saw carvings, mule rides, old gas and steam engine exhibits, and children's activities. A special treat is the Virginia Science Museum's Ocean in Motion, the museum's traveling aquarium. This program brings live animals and features tours of the truck and visits to the touching tanks.

Festival goers traverse Chippokes Plantation State Park in a wagon.
Courtesy of First Graphics, Inc.

Held the third weekend in July at 69 Chippokes Park Road.

URBANNA OYSTER FESTIVAL • URBANNA

"Give me oysters and beer every day of the year, and I'll be fine. ... I'll feel fiiine!" Guess Jimmy Buffett says it best when it comes to the succulent little bottom feeder. A little catsup. Some horseradish (lots of that) and an ice-cold beer. Life is good.

Begun in 1958 as Urbanna Days, this festival celebrates the town and its economy, which is strongly tied to the crops of oysters that reside in the bay. It was officially renamed the Urbanna Oyster Festival in 1961, and in 1988, the General Assembly of Virginia designated it as the official Oyster Festival of the Commonwealth.

Besides the eating of the wonderfully slimy bivalve, there's a traditional Friday night Fireman's Parade, featuring more than eighty fire engines, and a Saturday Oyster Festival Parade, featuring marching bands, antique cars, and floats.

The crowning of a queen and a Little Miss Spat (A spat is a baby oyster. Ain't that just so cute!) is also an important tradition. In addition, there are foods, crafts, and live entertainment. Hey, it's a festival that closes down the whole town! You just can't miss it.

Held in November.

Virginia Gourd Festival • Middletown

Now this is a strange but true festival. Every year the Virginia Chapter of the American Gourd Society (who knew—a whole society of gourds) sponsors a weekend of education and fun centered around these funny-looking, inedible vegetables. You can learn all about crafting gourds, from preparing to carving to fashioning them into fun items. There are classes on

A woman shops for gourds at the Virginia Gourd Festival. Courtesy of Norman and Mary Hooks

making a gourd maranka, a musical instrument made by netting beads around the outside of a gourd. The musical sound is made by shaking the gourd or sliding the beads against the surface. There are also classes in making such items as jewelry, gourd dishes, gourd art, and gourd ornaments. You can also enjoy live music and lots of good food.

Held in November at Richard's Fruit Market at 6410 Middle Road.

Whitetop Mountain Molasses Festival • Whitetop

Regardless of its name, this isn't a festival that moves as slow as mol…well, you know. Actually, it's quite an event, featuring live music with the region's best mountain music makers, dancing, food, and drink. You can also get up close and personal with molasses and apple butter making. And, as an added treat—the mountain foliage is in full color. So, don't forget the camera.

Held in October at the Mt. Rogers Fire Department on Route 58.

Close Encounters of the Virginia Kind

Virginia is a hotbed of UFO activity. From Danville to Marion, Crittendon to Williamsburg, and even at Langley Air Force Base, strange flying objects have been seen for decades in the starry Virginia sky.

For instance, according to Project Blue Book—the U.S. government department in charge of debunking UFO sightings—at 10:45 a.m. on August 23, 1955, Arlington resident G.M. Park, using a 400x telescope, saw several orange lights moving around the sky. Sometimes they moved singly, sometimes together, circling and stopping over a thirty-minute period.

Also in Arlington at 1:00 a.m. on a July 2002 morning, two witnesses, looking for a lost kitty, saw two baseball-sized lights fly over their house. Two minutes later, the objects came back, stopping to hover for a few seconds. Then one zoomed off at a right angle and disappeared over the horizon. The second object hovered for a few seconds longer. Then it, too, zoomed out of sight. No word on the lost kitty.

Strange But True Culture

Artists, world-class storytellers, music, and music men—it's culture with a twist in Strange But True Virginia.

Artists

Folk artists. Self-taught artists. Outsiders. Whatever you call them, it's been said that there's just one rule in folk art: The artists must be as interesting as their art. No problem here!

STEVE ASHBY

Hard times affect people differently. For some, the hard times become a hammer that beats them down. Others take that hammer and beat the hard times into art that touches the world.

Steve Ashby knew his share of hard times. Born in Delaplane, he lived his whole life in Fauquier Country, working as a farm hand, a hotel waiter, and a gardener. He dabbled in wood sculpting, but didn't take it up seriously until after the death of his wife in 1962.

Ashby's inspiration often hit him in his sleep, he said. Ideas woke him up and wouldn't let him go back to sleep. So he'd get up and "make that idea." Those ideas often translated into carvings of the rural activities of Fauquier County, where his ancestors had been slaves.

Ashby carved both small and life-sized human and animal figures, embellished with found objects. Since he was a man with a penchant for girlie magazines, his figures were often anatomically correct, with many bordering on pornographic. He often dressed up the life-sized human figures in various costumes and set them on a makeshift bench outside his home. Some figures were wind-activated and others had parts that moved when handled, such as his carving titled *Nodding Woman*, whose flexible saw-blade neck allowed her head to bob.

Ashby died in Delaplane in 1980.

Miles Carpenter

Miles Carpenter is considered one of the twentieth century's most important folk art carvers. He was born in Pennsylvania in 1889, but was reared in Waverly, where his father ran a sawmill. Carpenter took up the family business, running a sawmill from 1912 until 1957.

At age fifty, he began carving wood figures in the tradition of folk art, producing hand-painted carvings of animals, humans, and biblical characters. He enjoyed looking for the humor in natural objects, such as a piece of twisted driftwood, which he fashioned into a green and yellow frog toy. The distortion of the driftwood made it appear that the frog was walking forward on its front legs rather than leaping on its back legs. At his death in 1985, Carpenter was a nationally renowned folk artist.

Robert Howell

Sometimes a stack of wood is more than just splinters and kindling. Sometimes it's a whole pile of ideas. Powhatan County resident Robert Howell was a true outsider artist who could look at a piece of crooked wood and see what was inside it—a hitchhiker, his thumb hooked in the air; a mermaid with a flipping tail. A blue fish. An alligator. A whirligig. The Statue of Liberty.

A true outsider artist, Howell took those crooked pieces of wood, added the discards of the world—soda cans, carpeting, paper—and turned the yard of his tumbledown home into a fantastical landscape of humorous human and animal sculptures. He began making his art more than fifty years ago while working as a caretaker at an apartment complex in Richmond. He caught sight of a duck whirligig at a hardware store and decided to make one of his own. That first attempt, he said, wasn't much to look at, and he couldn't get its wings to spin in opposite directions, but making it sparked a creative fire.

For the next forty years, he used hatchets, hammers, nails, and other tools to fashion his work. His inventiveness and creativity set him apart from other folk artists. Because of an aversion to self-promotion, he's not as well-known as many of his peers, but his work is internationally known. Howell died in 2004 at the age of seventy-two.

S. L. Jones

Born in Franklin County, S.L. Jones was an accomplished fiddler by age ten. He also enjoyed hunting, and took to carving small wooden figures while waiting for deer. It wasn't until later life—after the death of his first wife—that he returned to his boyhood hobby. In the early 1970s, he began exhibiting his carvings of rabbits, dogs, and horses at county fairs, where he earned a reputation as a single image artist.

Best known for carved wood portrait heads, Jones draws and carves figures of people he has known or visions from his dreams. He whittles his carvings from maple, black walnut, and yellow poplar, embellishing them with paint. His drawings are in pencil or crayon. His work is displayed in the Smithsonian Institution in Washington, D.C., and the Museum of American Folk Art in New York City.

Music from the Heart

A huge portion of America's musical heritage emanated from the heart of Appalachia. Both country and bluegrass music were born here, products of traditional backwoods ballads, picked out on the front porches of Appalachian homes.

In addition, Virginia is the birthplace of musical greats in all genres: Pearl Bailey, Ella Fitzgerald, Kate Smith, Bruce Hornsby, Wayne Newton, Dave Matthews, and Missy Elliott, considered the top female hip-hop artist of all time.

Join us for a strange but true trek through the foothills of southwestern Virginia, down the historical trail now known as the Crooked Road, which snakes its way through 250 miles of back roads and foothills of nine southwestern Virginia counties. It's a magical tour through musical history.

Appalachian Music

Music has always been an integral part of life in Southern Appalachia. Songs that tell a story are the mainstay of the musical tradition. These ballads can be based on an event in history, humorous situations, tragedy, happiness, or the supernatural. Because most of the original settlers were unable to read, these oral traditions were used to teach history, morality, and the ethics of the community. Favorites include "Old Joe Clark," "Sourwood Mountain," and "Mister Frog Went A-Courtin'."

In addition to ballads, Southern Appalachia has strong instrumental music traditions, featuring such instruments as the mountain dulcimer, fiddle, banjo, and the limberjack.

In the 1920s, Appalachian music became known as "old-time" music, with mountain groups surprising urban record companies with the popularity of their string band music. Virginia performers, such as the Carter Family, and Carter and Ralph Stanley, were able to quit their day jobs and make a living from music. The boon was short-lived, however, with the Great Depression of the 1930s putting an end to the commercial viability of old-time music.

The music survives, though. You can hear it echoing from the mountain backwoods, livening folk music festivals, parties, and front-porch jams throughout Appalachia. Be lucky enough to attend one and you'll experience a Virginia unchanged by the centuries.

Pearl Bailey

Newport News's Pearl Bailey credited her love of music to her childhood experience as the daughter of a "Holy Roller" evangelical minister. She got her start in show business at age fifteen, when she won an amateur talent contest at the Pearl Theater in Philadelphia. After winning her second such contest—at Harlem's Apollo Theater—she decided to pursue a career in entertainment.

She began singing and dancing in black nightclubs in Philadelphia in the 1930s. It was here that she developed her throaty singing style, punctuated with humorous asides and ad-libs. During World War II, she toured with the USO, and then settled in New York, where she made her Broadway debut in 1946 in the show *St. Louis Woman*. As an actress, she was known for her charm and her comedic timing.

Throughout the 1950s and 1960s, Bailey toured and appeared regularly on television variety shows. She returned to Broadway in 1967, starring in an all-black version of *Hello, Dolly!*, for which she won a Tony Award.

Having achieved superstar status, Bailey was named a special delegate to the United Nations during the Reagan, Bush, and Clinton administrations. She retired from show business in 1975 and decided to complete her education. At age sixty-seven, she graduated from Georgetown University with a degree in theology. In 1988, she received the Presidential Medal of Freedom. Bailey died in 1990.

THE CARTER FAMILY

The Carter Family has been called the most influential group in country music history. Along with singer Jimmie Rodgers, they were the first country music stars. The original group was comprised of family patriarch Alvin P. Carter, who played fiddle and sang bass; his wife, Sara, who played the autoharp and sang alto lead; and sister-in-law "Mother" Maybelle Carter, who played guitar and sang harmony.

Formed in the 1920s, the group switched the emphasis from hillbilly instrumental music to vocals. The trio collected hundreds of British/Appalachian folk songs that had been played in the areas around their Clinch Mountain home, adding their sweet, simple harmonies, which enhanced the beauty of the songs and made them "Carter songs," regardless of the fact that they had been around for hundreds of years. Their classic recordings include "Wabash Cannonball," "Keep on the Sunny Side," "Will The Circle Be Unbroken," and "Worried Man Blues."

The Carter Family made their first recordings in Bristol on the Tennessee side of the street, as part of a recording call by Victor executive Ralph Peer. For the next seventeen years, they recorded more than three hundred songs in their unique style, including ballads, gospel hymns, and country songs. Their instrumental accompaniment was as unique as their vocals. Mother Maybelle, often referred to as the Queen of Country Music, had a distinctive method of guitar playing that became the mainstay of bluegrass guitarists.

By the 1930s, the Carter Family was the most bankable group in the country, with sales of more than a million. In the late 1930s, they began playing on the radio station XERA, which was broadcast from coast to coast. Throughout the country, a whole generation of future country music greats soaked in the Carters' harmonies from those broadcasts—

Johnny Cash, Waylon Jennings, Chet Atkins, and Tom T. Hall.

The original group broke up in the 1940s, but Mother Maybelle continued performing with her three daughters—Anita, Helen, and June, who later married Johnny Cash. Mother Maybelle and the Carter Sisters performed together from 1943 until 1946, first at radio stations in Richmond, then in Knoxville. Their final stop was the Grand Ole Opry in Nashville.

The Carter Family was inducted into the Country Music Hall of Fame in 1970, the first group to be given that honor. Their music has had a lasting influence, inspiring such diverse artists as Woody Guthrie, Bill Monroe, the Kingston Trio, Bob Dylan, and Emmylou Harris.

Roy Clark

By the age of fourteen, Virginia native Roy Clark was a consummate picker. No, he weren't out in the field pickin' peas. All his pickin' was done on the stage. Clark began playing the banjo, guitar, and mandolin at age fourteen, and by the time he was seventeen, he'd won two National Banjo Championships and had picked his way to an appearance on the Grand Ole Opry.

Blessed with an amiable personality and excellent comic timing, Clark pursued a show business career, pickin' and grinnin' his way through hit records, television appearances, and stage performances. In the 1950s, he was a regular on the *Jimmy Dean Show*, taking it over when Dean left. He frequently guest-hosted the *Tonight Show* and had a recurring role in the hit show

The Beverly Hillbillies. He's best known for cohosting (with Buck Owens) the first country music variety show, *Hee Haw*. Though the show lasted only three years, it ran in syndication for more then twenty years, delighting generations with its unique homespun humor.

Today, Clark is still pickin' and grinnin', primarily at the theater he owns in Branson, Missouri.

Ella Fitzgerald

Maybe it's something in the water in Newport News. This quintessential Virginia town was the birthplace of two of the country's biggest African-American musical talents: Pearl Bailey and Ella Fitzgerald. Lady Ella was the undisputed Queen of Jazz. Gifted with a three-octave vocal range that newsman David Brinkley said needed an elevator to go from the top to the bottom, she is known for her improvisational ability—a talent that served her best in scat singing.

Her career began at age sixteen, when, like Bailey, she won an amateur talent contest at the Apollo Theater. Fitzgerald recorded several hit records soon after, but was propelled to stardom by an unlikely song—her rendition of the nursery rhyme "A-Tisket, A-Tasket."

Throughout her long career, she sang all types of styles—scat, bebop, blues, bossa nova, samba, gospel, and calypso—with the most important bands and performers.

Wayne Newton

Who woulda thunk it? The same state that gave birth to bluegrass and country music is also the birthplace of Mr. Las

Vegas. It's not such a surprise to those of us who are of a certain age. We remember Wayne Newton as a fresh-faced young man with a velvet voice and a polite, slightly hayseed, manner—though that hayseed part may be due to the fact that our first glimpse of him was in the role of a country boy with a great voice on an *I Love Lucy* episode.

Back then, he really rocked with such hits as "Red Roses for a Blue Lady" and his signature hit, "Danke Shoen." Oh, relax. It means "thank you" in German. OK, so it wasn't exactly rock 'n' roll, but it was popular back in the day, and it made the young Roanoke native a national star.

Newton's interest in show biz began many years before those 1960s hits. He was just four when his parents took him to a performance of the Grand Ole Opry in Roanoke, and watching Hank Williams Jr. and Kitty Wells inspired him to his life's ambition. Luckily, he had the voice to back up his ambition, and before long, he was performing on stage. By the time he was six, he had performed for President Harry Truman in a USO show, and at eight won the chance to audition for the hit amateur talent show *Ted Mack's Original Amateur Hour*—which he lost. Didn't stop him, though.

By the 1970s, Newton began his Vegas career, starting out as a $1,500 a night opening act for Jack Benny. He loved it so much that when the gig was up and he was offered another opening-act stint, he asked to headline his own show, a request that was granted—with a catch. He was given a slot in November, the deadest month of the year in Las Vegas.

Everyone expected his act to flop, but the naysayers

hadn't counted on Newton's popularity with the locals. He set hotel attendance records, and set the stage for his ascent to the throne of the country's gaudiest city. Today, as Mr. Las Vegas, Newton has won so many Entertainer of the Year honors that it's been suggested that the title be retired. Bedecked in gold and sporting his signature pompadour, Newton packs 'em into the Stardust Resort's theater, now named the Wayne Newton Theater.

KATE SMITH

She was a big woman with a big voice. From an early age at her childhood home in Greenville, Kate Smith loved to sing and dance. She began performing locally in theaters and nightclubs until 1926, when she was discovered by a New York City producer.

In addition to appearing in Broadway musicals and movies, she began a recording career, producing hit after hit. She soon became America's most beloved entertainer. Although her theme song was "When the Moon Comes Over the Mountain," which she cowrote, her biggest hit was a little song by Irving Berlin titled "God Bless America." The song was so well loved that in 1938, Smith predicted it would still be sung long after she was gone. The fact that "God Bless America" is considered by many to be the second national anthem has proven that prediction to be accurate.

In an unusual twist at the end of her career, Smith became a singing lucky charm for the Philadelphia Flyers hockey team, who occasionally played her recording of "God Bless America" before a home game. The perception developed that when the song was played, the team won the game. It became a tradition to play the song, and several times—when the Flyers were in contention for the Stanley Cup—Smith appeared to sing the song live. She was credited with helping them win two consecutive Stanley Cups.

In 1982, Smith was awarded the Presidential Medal of Freedom by President Ronald Reagan. She died in Raleigh, North Carolina, on June 17, 1986.

Ralph and Carter Stanley

The Stanley brothers were a couple of good ol' Virginia mountain boys who liked to pick out a few songs on their front porch. Taking their mountain traditions, music, and songs, and weaving them into a new sound of simplicity and beauty, the brothers played a major role in the development of bluegrass music. Their traditional bluegrass sound paralleled the

Ralph and Carter Stanley perform at the 1964 Newport Folk Festival. Left to right: Ralph Stanley, George Shuffler, Carter Stanley, and Red Stanley (no relation).
Photo by John Byrne Cooke/www.cookephoto.com

music of bluegrass pioneers Flatt and Scruggs and Bill Monroe's Blue Grass Boys.

The Stanleys were born into a musical family—father sang...bass? And mama played banjo. It was mom, in fact, that taught the boys the distinctive clawhammer style of banjo picking for which they became famous. In 1946, the boys formed their first band, the Clinch Mountain Boys, and began appearing regularly on radio shows, where they gained a following.

In 1947, they signed a contract with the Rich-R-Tone recording label and made their first records. As the five-piece band traveled around the South, appearing at various radio stations, their style evolved from traditional string sounds to the more ultra-traditional bluegrass style made popular by Bill Monroe and the Blue Grass Boys.

In 1948, the band signed with Columbia Records, a relationship that lasted three years. The twenty-two songs they recorded here defined the Stanleys' approach to bluegrass, with their haunting mountain melodies setting them apart from other artists. These recordings have become bluegrass classics.

When Carter died at the age of forty-one, Ralph carried on. His ability to hit the right notes and chords gave his vocals a mournful "high lonesome" sound that drew people from California to the hollers of Kentucky. His music inspired such artists as Dwight Yoakam, Emmylou Harris, and Ricky Skaggs. Both Carter and Ralph are members of the Bluegrass Hall of Fame.

Writers

No doubt about it, Virginia is a hotbed of literary talent, with Pulitzer Prize winners galore. There's political columnist Russell Baker, historian William Bruce, novelist Willa Cather, historian Virginius Dabney, biographer Douglas Freeman, novelist Ellen Glasgow, poet Rita Dove, and novelist William Styron. Whew! That's quite a list.

It's not the complete list, though. Oh, no, not by any means. These folks may not have won any Pulitzers, but so what? They've got a much more interesting honor: They've been deemed worthy of our Strange But True Virginia tour!

Rita Mae Brown

Where do we start? How about with Rita Mae Brown's activism? She was kicked out of the University of Florida in 1964 for her participation in a civil rights rally, after which she hitchhiked to New York and lived for a time in an abandoned car with a gay African-American and a cat named Baby Jesus. She soon enrolled in New York University, where she earned a degree in the Classics and English, and also started the Student Homophile League, a group that represented gay students. Oh, did we forget to mention that Brown is gay?

The success of Brown's first book, *Rubyfruit Jungle*, a semi-autobiographical novel, proved to publishers that there was a market for lesbian fiction. Its popularity made her a spokesperson for gay and lesbian issues. In addition to writing best-selling fiction, Brown also has a quite lucrative career as a screenwriter. That was, in fact, her main income for a time.

OK, so that's interesting info about Rita Mae Brown, who lives in Charlottesville, but it's not what gets her on our Strange But True tour. As far as we're concerned, the most interesting thing about Brown is Sneaky Pie Brown, her real-life literary companion, who writes mystery novels. Did we mention that Sneaky Pie Brown is a cat? True, Brown is the one doing the typing, but it's Sneakie Pie who devises the plot and tells her what to type.

The collaboration came about in 1988, when a Writer's Guild strike threatened Brown's finances. Sneakie Pie, worried about where the next bowl of kibble was coming from, suggested they write mystery novels, a genre Brown had vowed never to dabble in. Sneakie Pie insisted, however, pointing out that though the money had dried up, the bills were still flowing freely.

As a result, the two now collaborate on a successful series of mysteries starring their alter egos, Mary Minor "Harry" Harrigan and Mrs. Murphy, a tiger tabby. Set in Crozet, Virginia, where Harry is postmaster, the novels feature a whole cast of zany characters, including doggy sleuth Tee Tucker, a corgi. They're great fun, and due to their popularity, Sneakie Pie no longer worries where her next meal is coming from.

PATRICIA CORNWELL

Getting sick off all those forensic shows featuring gory autopsies and yucky bodily fluid evidence? Well, blame Patricia Cornwell. Back in 1990, Cornwell wrote her first novel, a story about Kay Scarpetta, a fictional Richmond medical examiner who solves crimes by examining the forensic evidence. Titled *Postmortem*, it's the only novel ever to win the Edgar, Creasey, Anthony, Macavity, and the French Prix du Roman d'Aventure awards in one year. Her subsequent Scarpetta novels have all become national and international best-sellers, and many credit Cornwell with starting the current craze of forensic shows.

EDGAR ALLAN POE

No doubt about it, EAP was strange but true. Reportedly given to bouts of melancholy and madness, his work reflected his state of mind. The master of the macabre, Poe developed the modern horror story and is credited with inventing the detective story with his "Murders at the Rue Morgue."

Edgar Allan Poe is considered one of the greatest American writers.
Courtesy of the Edgar Allan Poe Museum, Richmond, VA

Poe's gloominess may have stemmed from the fact that he was orphaned before age three. He was taken into the home of Richmond native John Allan, whose wife, Francis, had cared for Poe's mother on her sickbed. Allan was not keen on the idea of taking Edgar in, and by all accounts, his support was grudging. Poe seemed hurt by the lack of affection afforded him by the wealthy tobacco businessman, taking the man's last name as his middle name when Allan refused to adopt him.

Their relationship was a stormy one, with Allan refusing to pay Poe's gambling debts, which Poe said he racked up because Allan was stingy. The hostility grew, and Allan eventually disowned Poe, who wrote a conciliatory letter, practically begging Allan for his financial help. Allan returned the letter to him inscribed "Pretty Letter."

Poe published his first book of poems in 1827. The book did not sell well then, but has become one of the most prized collector's items today. After winning $50 in a writing contest for his story "MS Found in a Bottle," he began a career as a staff member for several magazines, including the Richmond *Southern Literary Messenger*, Philadelphia's *Burton's Gentleman's Magazine*, and *Graham's Magazine*, where he wrote many of his best stories.

During this time, he was leading a reckless life, often wandering the streets drunk, and often assuming a false identity to avoid creditors. In 1836, he married Virginia Clemm, his thirteen-year-old cousin (shades of Jerry Lewis!), and may have rallied for a time. But in 1842, Clemm, who suffered from tuberculosis, soon became an invalid, and after her death in 1847, Poe began a deep descent into alcoholism and drug addiction, facts reflected strongly in his stories and poems.

Poe's work is a study in the darkness of the mind. His poems of lost love, such as "Annabel Lee," about Clemm, and "The Raven" reflect one of his favorite subjects—the death of a beautiful woman. His short stories, such as "The Fall of the

House of Usher" and "The Tell-Tale Heart," all involve horror, death, madness, and gloom. Wes Craven's got nothing on Poe.

Poe's death at age forty was as mysterious and depressing as his work. On October 3, 1849, he was found wandering the streets of Baltimore, delirious and dressed in clothes that weren't his own. He'd been missing from Richmond for three days. Taken to a Baltimore hospital, he never regained consciousness to explain where he'd been or how he got there. He died on October 7, uttering the last words, "It's all over now. Write [on his tombstone] 'Eddy is no more.'"

Richmond's Poe Museum opened in 1922 in The Old Stone House, at 1914-16 East Main Street, just blocks away from Poe's first Richmond home and his first place of employment, the *Southern Literary Messenger*, where he served as editor.

Here you can see one of the largest collections of Poe memorabilia in the world, which includes many arcane items of Poe's dark life.

Inventors

From steamboats to abdominal surgery, Virginians are an inventive group. Here just a few of them and their creations or discoveries.

Cyrus McCormick

Cyrus McCormick's invention is credited with transforming our society from a farming country to the most powerful industrial nation in the world. OK, maybe that's overstating it a bit, but not much.

At the age of fifteen, McCormick conceived plans for a machine-driven grain reaper. He built it, tested it, and refined it, all within six weeks—just in time for the 1831 harvest. By 1834, he had patented his design and was selling more than he could produce at Walnut Grove, his Augusta County farm.

In 1847, McCormick moved to Chicago to take advantage of its proximity to the vast Midwestern prairie fields. Here, he proved he was not only mechanically inclined, but also innovative in business and marketing practices. By pioneering such business techniques as easy credit to enable farmers to pay for the machines from their increased harvests, written performance guarantees, and advertising, McCormick vastly increased the popularity of his Virginia Reaper, which won the 1851 Gold Medal at London's Crystal Palace Exhibition, the highest honor of the day. McCormick became a world celebrity.

Thanks to the efficiency provided by the reaper and other farm machines built at McCormick's company, formerly International Harvester and now Tenneco's J.I. Case affiliate, we have been transformed from a bucolic populace, where 90 percent of us farmed the land, to an urban rat race, where 98 percent of us sell our souls to make a living. Thanks a lot, Cyrus.

Ephraim McDowell

Ephraim McDowell, born in Rockbridge County, was known as the Father of Abdominal Surgery. He performed the first ovary removal in the United States in 1809, and although this was some feat, we think perhaps the most heroic person here must be patient Jane Crawford, who underwent the procedure without benefit of anesthesia, which hadn't been invented yet. McDowell's most famous patient was President James Polk, for whom he removed a gall stone and repaired a hernia.

Ironically, McDowell died in 1830 with an acute attack of violent stomach pain, nausea, and fever—most likely appendicitis. Guess that's the problem with being the first—no one else around to perform the surgery on you!

Walter Reed

Walter Reed was born and reared in Belroi, Virginia. After graduating from the University of Virginia, he became a medical officer with the U.S. Army at a time when widespread acceptance of Louis Pasteur's germ theory was transforming the practice of medicine. Reed worked closely with George Sternberg, the Army Surgeon General, who was one of the founders of bacteriology.

Walter Reed proved that yellow fever is transmitted by mosquitoes.
Courtesy of Historical Collections & Services, Claude Moore Health Sciences Library, University of Virginia

In May 1900, the Army appointed Reed president of a board whose task it was to study infectious diseases in Cuba, particularly yellow fever. Yellow fever had become a huge problem for the Army during the Spanish American War, where it had killed thousands of soldiers. It had also stopped the construction of the Panama Canal thirty years before.

Reed's team proved Dr. Carlos Finlay's theory that yellow fever is transmitted by mosquitoes rather than through direct contact. Their work disproved the common belief that the disease was spread through contact with bedding and clothing soiled by bodily fluids and excrement of yellow fever sufferers. It's mostly due to this discovery that the Panama Canal was finally completed.

Reed died of peritonitis following an appendectomy (those appendixes sure are dangerous) in 1902 and was buried in Arlington Cemetery. He was awarded the Walter Reed Medal posthumously for his work in discovering the cause of yellow fever.

James Rumsey

On December 3, 1787, James Rumsey of Bath, Virginia (now Berkeley Springs, West Virginia), debuted his design of the first steamboat, a feat that so impressed a group of Philadelphians, including one Ben Franklin, that they immediately formed the Rumsian Society as a way to publicize Rumsey's invention. The men encouraged Rumsey to travel to England to secure patents and seek further backing, which he promptly did.

Rumsey spent four years in England, where he improved on his design and built a new and improved steamboat, the *Columbia*

Maid. On December 20, 1792, on the eve of the demonstration of the *Columbia Maid*, Rumsey was suddenly struck with severe head pain. He died the next day. At that time, his death was attributed to overstraining his brain. Huh. If that could kill ya, we woulda been dead a long time ago. Can you say stroke?

Strange But True Song Status

"Carry Me Back to Old Virginny" was written by African-American minstrel James Bland, and has been Virginia's state song since 1940. On January 28, 1997, the Virginia Senate voted 24-15 to designate the classic as the "state song emeritus," and appointed a committee to study the adoption of a new state song. Three hundred and thirty-nine entries were received. Fifty-nine semi-finalists soon became twenty finalists. Eight grand finalists were named in July 1999. But in January 2000, the work of the State Song Subcommittee was temporarily suspended. A date for resuming the process has not been set.

Historical Events Around Virginia

What better way to learn about history than to be right in the middle of it! See it unfold before your eyes at one of these events.

American Revolution Reenactments

As the Birthplace of the Nation, Virginia played an integral role in this country's fight for independence. Reliving those important battles reminds us of the price we paid and fills us with patriotic pride. The following is just a sample of the battle reenactments that take place every year.

Reenactors prepare to fight the British in the Battle of Green Spring.
Courtesy of Todd Post/2d Regiment

Battle of Green Spring

Talk about good ol' American ingenuity and guts. General Anthony Wayne, whose nickname Mad Anthony may well have been earned at the Battle of Green Spring, had it in spades.

It was June 1781, and British General Charles Cornwallis was facing disappointment in Virginia. His campaign to capture the state had left British forces in the Carolinas weak and on the defensive, and now he was being ordered to New York without a decisive victory.

As July approached and Cornwallis was abandoning Williamsburg, he decided to try one last-ditch effort to lure Generals Lafayette and Wayne into a major battle. Concealing most of his army along the shore of the James River, he hoped to trick Lafayette into believing that only a small rear guard remained. To reinforce the ruse, he sent two "deserters" to confirm that the bulk of the British army had already left.

Lafayette fell for the ruse, sending Mad Anthony and a troop of eight hundred to face a force of five thousand. Wayne, recognizing the situation, tried to confuse Cornwallis by sending marksmen forward, also sending runners back to inform Lafayette of the situation. Cornwallis, no slouch in the confusing tactics department, wasn't fooled and began to advance. Realizing he'd be quickly overwhelmed, Wayne decided on another ruse. He organized a bayonet charge. Now that was one Cornwallis didn't expect. Believing no one would order such an attack without the forces to back it up, Cornwallis broke off his advance and moved on to Portsmouth. Although the battle, the last major battle of the Virginia campaign before the siege of Yorktown, was technically a loss, the fact that Lafayette kept his force intact to battle another day was a major factor in deciding the fate of the war.

Reenactments of the Battle of Green Spring bring the battle to life periodically. There are encampments and demonstrations that portray the everyday life of colonial soldiers and civilians. Held in Williamsburg.

Battle of Yorktown

The British loss at Yorktown, essentially the end of the Revolutionary War, came about because of American tenacity and several critical mistakes by British General Charles Cornwallis. There were several key battles that Cornwallis technically won, but in which he experienced heavy losses that battered his troops.

Following the March 15, 1781, Battle at Guilford Court House in North Carolina, another of those battles he won at a heavy cost, he disobeyed orders from his commander to stay put and protect North Carolina. Instead, he moved on to Virginia, where after more technical wins with heavy losses, he moved into Yorktown.

Yorktown battlefield is the site of British surrender.
Courtesy of Colonial Historic National Park/VTC

Hearing of Cornwallis's encampment in Yorktown, Washington abandoned plans to attack New York and hurried to Virginia, arriving in time to bottle up Cornwallis and his troops, with the help of the French fleet in Chesapeake Bay.

The British fleet sailed from New York in an attempt to rescue Cornwallis, but it was too late. On October 19, 1781, Cornwallis surrendered his army. Well, he called in sick and had his second-in-command surrender. Remember, we told that story already. Upon hearing of the defeat, British Prime Minister Frederick Lord North said, "Oh, God, it's all over." And it was. Seems Cornwallis had won the battles but lost the war.

The Battle of Yorktown is commemorated periodically with reenactments and living history demonstrations.

Crossing of the Dan River

Despite the fact that General Nathanael Greene's crossing of the Dan River in February 1781 was made in retreat, it was a pivotal event in the American Revolution. The events leading up to the crossing began a month earlier, when British General Banastre Tarleton was soundly defeated by Brigadier General Daniel Morgan at Cowpens, North Carolina. Morgan had been leading a small contingent of Greene's troops, and following the Battle of Cowpens, he rejoined Greene and his main force, and began a retreat to the Dan River on the border of North Carolina and Virginia.

The retreat, which became known as the Race to the Dan, was accomplished in one month, with troops marching the two hundred miles through rainy weather that turned the roads to mud and swelled rivers and streams. Cornwallis pursued, hoping to catch Greene and force major battle, for which he knew Greene was ill prepared.

In his hasty pursuit, Cornwallis burned his baggage train, overextended his supply lines, and left his army strung out for miles. In an attempt to deceive Cornwallis, Greene once again split his troops, sending a small contingent north to cover the retreat of the larger army. Cornwallis, unaware that Greene had arranged for boats to carry his troops across the river, assumed that he would cross at a shallower point, fell for the ruse, and decided to follow the small contingent.

That decision decided the fate of the war, for had he caught Greene and destroyed his troops, North Carolina would have been in British hands, with Virginia not far behind. By the time he discovered his mistake, Greene's troops were across the Dan, thumbing their noses at the British, prompting Cornwallis to say of his wily opponent, "Greene is more dangerous than Washington. I never feel secure when camped in his neighborhood."

The Crossing of the Dan was considered a major feat by Greene, whom many rated second only to George Washington in military strategy. The event is celebrated in February in South Boston (Virginia) every year. There are reenactments, a living history encampment on the banks of the Dan, period music, and a live appearance by General Greene on his horse, MacAwesome. Uh-huh. We're gonna assume these two are actors.

Civil War Reenactments

Virginia has more Civil War reenactments than Carter's got liver pills. Could it be we think if we keep redoing it, one day we'll chase those damn Yankees back over the Mason-Dixon Line? Nah. It's just a good excuse to dress up in old clothes and play soldier. Here's just a mere sample of the state's yearly reenactments.

Battle of Big Bethel

Hee-hee. Don't you just love it when the enemy's plan backfires? That's just what happened in this battle—the first Virginia land battle of the Civil War.

It all started with the arrival of Union General Benjamin Franklin Butler at Fort Monroe on the southern tip of the Virginia peninsula. The Rebs, twenty-five thousand strong, had already arrived, working for two days to build a solid earthwork defensive position at the small village of Big Bethel, just eight miles from Fort Monroe.

Having the enemy in such close proximity made Butler nervous. So, he came up with a plan for a sneak attack. Dividing his troops of forty-four hundred into two columns, he sent them on a night march, with the idea to meet and surprise the Rebs. To really confuse the Rebs, Butler had dressed some of the soldiers in one column in gray uniforms and came up with "Boston" as a password for the guys in gray to identify themselves to the other column as friendlies. However, somehow that information never got passed on to the second column. Oops.

In the pre-dawn hours of June 10, the two columns came together. One column, seeing gray uniforms, thought the jig was up and began firing. They continued firing, perhaps wondering why all those Rebs were screaming "Boston" at them. The two Union regiments in front thought they were being attacked from the rear and retreated. The attackers realized their mistake—after inflicting twenty-one casualties—and the two columns backed off and regrouped.

With the element of surprise now gone, they attacked the Rebs with twenty-five hundred men. There were eighteen men killed, fifty-three wounded, and five missing. Meanwhile, the Rebs, happily ensconced in their bulwarks, lost only one soldier and had only seven wounded. They had engaged only twelve hundred soldiers. After an hour of fighting, the Yankees broke off and returned to Fort Monroe, their tails tucked between their legs. Ha!

The Battle of Big Bethel is reenacted annually with more than one thousand reenactors taking the field. Held in March at the Endview Plantation in Newport News, there are also ladies' activities, live entertainment, children's activities, lectures, and demonstrations.

Located at 362 Yorktown Road, Newport News.

Battle of Hampton Roads

In March 1862, Chesapeake Bay was filled with Union ships that were slowly strangling the Confederacy. All that was about to change, however, in a history-making event that rendered wooden warships practically obsolete.

Departing from Norfolk on March 8, 1862, the Confederate's ironclad boat, the *Virginia,* attacked the Union blockade of ships, and within fifteen minutes of firing the first shot, rammed and sank the twenty-four-gun *Cumberland*. She then attacked the fifty-gun frigate the *Congress*, which fought valiantly, only to see its shells bounce harmlessly off the *Virginia*'s iron hull. Within an hour, her decks drenched in blood, the *Congress* surrendered and was burned by the crew of the *Virginia*.

The *Virginia* returned to Norfolk overnight, returning the next morning expecting a repeat of the previous day's victory. Didn't happen. Upon approaching the fifty-gun *Minnesota*, the *Virginia* found her protected by the Union's own ironclad, the *Monitor*. The ensuing battle, considered historical because it was the first meeting of ironclads, ended in a stalemate, with neither able to penetrate the other's ironclad defenses

The Battle of Hampton Roads is celebrated annually with a weekend of Civil War encampments, tours of the Mariner's Museum, and other activities. Held at the Mariner's Museum at 100 Museum Drive in Newport News.

HUNTER'S RAID

In 2005, a new Virginia Civil War Trail opened to highlight the 1864 Virginia raid of Union General David Hunter. The trail, a driving tour connecting localities that experienced action during Hunter's Raid, winds through some of the most scenic Virginia countryside.

Hunter's Raid began in June, when General Ulysses Grant ordered Hunter and his troops to leave West Virginia and head for Lynchburg, an important Confederate supply and transportation center whose capture might hasten the end of the war. The first battle of the raid was at Piedmont on June 5. They marched on to Staunton, where numerous government buildings were burned. Next came Lexington, where they burned Virginia Military Institute and looted Washington College. They moved on to Natural Bridge, through Buchanan, the Peaks of Otter, Bedford, and New London, burning and skirmishing with Confederate troops all along the way.

Virginia Military Institute was burned during Hunter's Raid.
Courtesy of the Lexington & Rockbridge Area Tourism Development

The raid culminated with the Battle of Lynchburg on June 17 and 18, but it didn't quite end the way the Yankees had hoped. They were soundly defeated by Confederate troops led by General Jubal Early. The Rebs chased them Yankees back through Bedford and then to Salem, where they fought again in the Battle of Hanging Rock, another sound defeat for the blue coats.

In addition to the Civil War Trail following Hunter's route, there are periodic reenactments of the battles of Hunter's Raid, which include military encampments, performances of period music, Civil War field surgery, and period wedding and church services. Civil War celebrities, such as General Robert E. Lee, often make appearances.

Laurel Hill Encampment

Billed as one of the highest quality reenactment events in the world, the Laurel Hill Encampment brings the battles of the Civil War back to life. For just a short time, the thunder of big guns and the rattle of sabers once again ring through the Blue Ridge Mountains.

As the birthplace of Confederate Major General James Ewell Brown (JEB) Stuart, one of the greatest soldiers ever to wield a sword, Laurel Hill is listed on both the Virginia Landmark Register and the National Register of Historic Places. Each year, a series of Civil War battles are reenacted, including an appearance by JEB himself, a candlelight tour of the horrors of war, Civil War sutlers, and nineteenth-century music.

Reenactments are held at Laurel Hill, 1091 Arafat Highway, Arafat, Virginia.

Battle of Waynesboro

There are yearly reenactments of the Battle of Waynesboro, one of the last battles of the Civil War. You can tour the streets that now cover the battlegrounds and talk with reenactors, who tell you of the battle—a Confederate loss. The Plumb House, which was caught between battle lines, is open for tours and special exhibitions.

Held at the Plumb House at 1021 West Main Street.

Living History Events

See history unfold before you as you visit one of these living history sites.

COLONIAL WILLIAMSBURG

Talk about living history! Living in Williamsburg is living in history. The town, originally named Middle Plantation, was founded in 1632. Renamed Williamsburg in honor of England's King William III, it was made the state capital in 1699, when Jamestown burned.

As one of the thirteen original colonies, Virginia was rich and powerful. Stretching west to the Mississippi River and north to the Great Lakes, it was the most influential of the colonies. As its capital, Williamsburg was a political, cultural, and educational center at a time when the fundamental concepts of our country were being developed. Patriots George Washington, Thomas Jefferson, and George Mason

At the Peyton Randolph site in Colonial Williamsburg, historic trade carpenters reconstruct eight outbuildings that comprise Randolph's "urban plantation."
Courtesy of The Colonial Williamsburg Foundation/Williamsburg Area CVB

trod the cobblestones, espousing the ideals our country are founded upon—personal and religious freedom, responsible government, and equality of all.

In 1780, the capital was moved to Richmond, and Williamsburg, home to the College of William and Mary, became a quiet college town for the next 150 years. In 1926, the Reverend W.A.R. Goodwin, rector of the Bruton Parish Church, became concerned about losing the historical buildings of Williamsburg. Teaming with philanthropist John D. Rockefeller, he set about reconstructing, restoring, and preserving those buildings that played such an important role in our country's history. Together, they reconstructed more than 85 percent of the eighteenth-century capital's original area.

Today, that reconstructed area, Colonial Williamsburg, encompassing 301 acres and featuring hundreds of restored and reconstructed buildings, constitutes the world's largest living history museum. Daily, costumed interpreters tell the Colonial Williamsburg story—a story of how diverse peoples with different, sometimes conflicting, goals, evolved into a society that values liberty and equality.

The interpreters cover all points of view—black, white, Native American, free, slave, and indentured servants—and the challenges each faced. As you walk through Colonial Williamsburg, you step into the most exciting, glorious time of our history. Meet and talk with the country's first leaders: George Washington, Thomas Jefferson, and Patrick Henry. You can also talk with everyday citizens—from shopkeepers to slaves to the town's prominent families—and see how they lived. Learn about the lives of colonial children and enjoy the music of the Fife & Drums, an important part of colonial life.

Native Virginian Thomas Jefferson accomplished much in his lifetime. He served as governor of Virginia, U.S. minister to France, secretary of state under George Washington, vice president to John Adams, and finally, president of the United States. There are only three accomplishments for which he wanted to be remembered, however. In his own epitaph he wrote: "Here was buried Thomas Jefferson, author of the Declaration of Independence, of the Statute of Virginia for religious freedom, the Father of the University of Virginia."

Martin's Station

Martin's Station played a significant role in the history of Virginia. The station is named for its founder, Joseph Martin, whose 1769 expedition through the wilderness was the first to reach Powell's Valley.

The group laid claim to a tract of land near the present-day village of Rose Hill, where they carved a settlement out of the wilderness, erecting a fort and several crude cabins, and planting a crop of corn. Their attempts at settlement proved fruitless, when a Native American attack resulted in abandonment.

Martin retained his claim on the land, and in 1775, he returned with a group of eighteen men. They rebuilt the cabins and surrounded them with a stockade. As the last fortified station along the Wilderness Road, Martin's Station became an important stop for early settlers traveling to new lands in Kentucky.

Today, you can tour Martin's Station and take a step back to Virginia's wilderness days. History comes alive as more than 150 historians reenact life at the early Martin's Station, including the Native American attack that destroyed the first station. Watch as early Native Americans burn a cabin and tour Native American warrior and colonial militia camps. There are reenactments of the frontier life, and eighteenth-century vendors and colonial traders selling their wares.

Living history participants at Martin's Station reenact a Native American raid.
Photo by Mike Brindle, Wilderness Road State Park, Ewing, VA

Located at the Wilderness Road State Park in Ewing.